COACHING

THE BASIC
COACHING METHOD

Andy Buck

First Published 2020
Cadogan Press

© 2020 Andy Buck

All rights reserved.

No part of this publication may be reproduced, stored in a retrieval system, transmitted in any form or by any means, electronic, mechanical, photocopying, recording, or otherwise, without the prior permission of the publishers. Opinions expressed in this publication are those of the contributors and are not necessarily those of the publishers or the editors. We cannot accept responsibility for any errors or omissions.

ISBN: 978 1 912906 17 8

Set and designed by Cadogan Press
Printed by Book Printing UK

For my Uncle Peter

It was a pleasure reading this book. Andy Buck's voice and expertise really shine through. He offers practical insights (just enough) to show that he's *been there done that*. As someone who has been coached a few times, I really like the blended approach this coaching method offers, from traditional to instructional coaching and everything in between.

Tricia Taylor
Founder and Director, TailoredPractice

I love this book! The instructional coaching approach is a great way to assist colleagues who require a little more of a *hands-on* approach during coaching. I firmly believe this approach will really increase the self-capacity of coachees to self-reflect, become more decisive and increase their ability to engage in a highly beneficial coaching relationship. It's like learning to ride a bike and removing the support wheels when the time is right.

Gen Mitchell
Former Head of International Secondary School Berlin

Humble, honest and helpful, BASIC coaching is so much more than just another book on coaching. It pulls together numerous strategies readers will already be familiar with and reconsiders them through the lens of a coach. Andy distils his considerable experience of coaching and working in schools into a powerful and easily accessible tool for anyone interested in forming better relationships: professional or personal. Whether you are new to coaching or a trained coach, I would recommend that you add this book to your library.

Roger Higgins
Director of Norwich Research School, Notre Dame High School, Norwich

This was a brilliant book when I read an early draft so I can't wait to get my hands on the final version! If you are new to coaching or an established coach, this book is for you! Clear, concise, common sense and great to read cover to cover or dip into when you need a refresher. As someone who has had training as a coach and practiced coaching this book is still so valuable as a reminder and refresher of the skills and a confirmation of the elements of good coaching. I know this is a book I will continue to return to.

Lorna Good
Teacher, coach and parent.

This is a clearly structured, thoughtfully presented and focussed explanation of a method of coaching which has something to offer readers of all levels of experience. Andy takes a practical rather than theoretical approach, but the strategies he suggests are firmly rooted in research and his extensive professional experience. Suggested questions for coachees, prompts to aid reflection and additional resources are helpfully included at the end of every chapter. Andy explores how to coach, mentor, model and guide, offering advice where appropriate so that the person being supported feels clearer and more positive about the future as a result.

This is a book to dip into, using as you feel appropriate to your needs and the needs of those you are helping, whether in a professional or a personal context. The book presents a clear model for the coaching/coachee relationship and dialogue, but Andy encourages you to be flexible and adapt it according to your requirements and specific context: this is, as he says, "a useful framework, not a straitjacket". This is well worth the investment of your time!

Jill Berry
Former head, now leadership consultant

Andy Buck has done it again! With his characteristic precision and clarity, his new book BASIC provides you with simple tools that will promote productive and thought-provoking conversations at work, at home or as a professional coach. Every school and college leader, executive, manager or parent will learn something helpful and positive from the tips, tools and the structured approach that the BASIC method provides. As a result, you can look forward to deepening your relationships with family, friends and colleagues.

Mike Buchanan
CEO of Positively Leading

Some people just get it. They are able to explain the heart of a situation and unravel the mystery. Andy Buck gets it! I have been formally coaching for over a decade. I read this book and realised that there is more to learn, and my practice is about to change. Read the book, implement the techniques, find your own fabulous coaching self as you help others to become masters at relationship building. Recommendation? That implies buying this book is still optional. It's not. Get the book and change!

Diana Osagie
Director of Courageous Leadership

In *BASIC Coaching* Andy Buck has achieved what I thought would have been impossible! He has produced a book which can be equally helpful to staff and leaders in schools and academies, in business and any other organisation and in families. Grounded in research, *BASIC Coaching* offers, in a readable way, guidance which contains models, templates and questions which can support emotionally intelligent and purposeful conversation in a wide range of settings. I cannot recommend this book too strongly.

Tony Glover
Education consultant, former secondary head and National Leader of Education

ANDY BUCK

Author, speaker, former headteacher and director at the National College, now the CEO of Leadership Matters, creator of the BASIC coaching method and founder of The StARTed Foundation.

A geography teacher by trade, Andy went on to become a headteacher for thirteen years at two schools in east London. In his second headship, his school was judged outstanding and he was designated a National Leader of Education. In 2009, he was appointed a director at the National College for School Leadership and in 2012 was made Managing Director at one of the largest academy groups in the UK.

Andy subsequently founded Leadership Matters which aims to improve educational outcomes for pupils by supporting great leadership development. He has written extensively on leadership and coaching, including the best-selling *Leadership Matters*.

In 2018, Andy was invited to become a Founding Fellow of the College of Teaching and in 2019 established The StARTed Foundation, which aims to support young talent in the performing arts.

Andy's published books include:
+ Making School Work (2007)
+ What Makes a Great School? (2009)
+ What Makes a Great Middle Leader? Handbook for Middle Leaders (2014)
+ What Makes Great Middle Leadership? Handbook for Senior Leaders (2015)
+ Leadership Matters 3.0 (2018)
+ Honk! When teams come together, organisations fly (2019)
+ BASIC Coaching: An Introduction to the BASIC Coaching Model (2020)

Introduction..11

BASIC Overview..29

Part A:	**BASIC Steps**	
Chapter 1	BASIC Background	39
Chapter 2	BASIC Aim	51
Chapter 3	BASIC Strategy	59
Chapter 4	BASIC Implementation	71
Chapter 5	BASIC Commitment	81

Part B	**BASIC qualities**	
Chapter 6	Build Trust	89
Chapter 7	Remain Curious	99
Chapter 8	Show Empathy	109
Chapter 9	Stay Positive	119

Part C	**BASIC Habits**	
Chapter 10	Ask First	129
Chapter 11	Frame Well	141
Chapter 12	Listen Hard	151
Chapter 13	Play Back	161

Part D	**BASIC Feedback**	
Chapter 14	Make Connections	169
Chapter 15	Feed Forward	179

Final Thoughts...187

Recommended Reading..191

Acknowledgements..195

Introduction

I thought I'd begin this book with a story about my uncle.

Over the course of the last few weeks I've spent quite a lot of time having conversations with my Uncle Peter. When my father passed away three years ago, I effectively became my uncle's next-of-kin and the person he inevitably turns to when he needs help. He is fiercely independent and has lived alone very successfully in a two-bedroom flat in West Sussex for the last 20 years.

But his eyesight has gradually been deteriorating and his whole way of life is becoming increasingly difficult. He is also someone who really doesn't like change. Helping him to see that he may need to accept help from others on a daily basis, with having a hot meal at lunchtime for example, has been a real struggle. As I sit here reflecting on the last few weeks, I can see there have definitely been some conversations which have gone better than others.

The best conversations have ended with my Uncle Peter feeling really happy about the next steps we have agreed to take together. He has felt a sense of ownership and involvement. In contrast, other conversations haven't gone so well and have ended with me feeling rather frustrated and my Uncle Peter feeling like I have been badgering him, which has inevitably brought out his stubborn side.

So, what has been the difference? Where the conversations have gone really well, I have given my uncle the time and space to think about his situation, decide what he wants to change or achieve, talk through the possible choices, and then helped him to decide what he wants to do. In summary, I have been asking open questions, listening hard, playing back what he has said and enabling him to make his own decisions.

 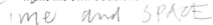

When the conversations haven't gone so well, my approach was equally well-meaning but instead of leaving Peter with a sense of ownership, greater clarity and a more optimistic outlook, it probably felt to him as if I was bullying him into doing something he didn't want to do.

Lessons learned

So, what can we learn from this example? Well, although these conversations are between an uncle and his nephew, the principles that underpin the differences between the more successful conversations and those that didn't go so well are equally applicable to interactions we may have with colleagues at work as well as with our friends and family. As you will have no doubt have already spotted, the conversations with my Uncle Peter that went well are effectively examples of me taking more of a coaching approach in the way I handled them.

But the use of coaching in the workplace can be equally as effective. I can remember one conversation with a coachee who at the start of the conversation, in response to the question: 'What's on your mind?' said there wasn't really anything that she was worried about.

By the end of the coaching session, simply by working through the BASIC coaching method, she had realised she needed to restructure her top team and was leaving the conversation with a five-step plan to make this happen. What is even more interesting is that neither of us had any inkling that this is where she would take the conversation. It's a great example of why trusting the coaching process itself to deliver results is so powerful.

The approach of this book

This is not an academic review of the field of coaching, although it is absolutely rooted in that research. Do take a look at the further reading listed at the end of each chapter if you are interested in learning more about the theory and thinking which this book draws from.

We know that using a coaching approach to conversations can make a huge difference to how productive they are, not just in the workplace but also in our lives more generally. However, the challenge is knowing exactly how to have them. What this book does is take the latest thinking and research from the field of coaching and translate it into the tried and tested BASIC method, which is easy to learn and simple to apply. This method offers you a powerful way to structure your conversations and outlines the essential skills you need to communicate effectively.

Over the last eight years I have had the privilege and pleasure of working with a number of inspirational coaching trainers and thought leaders. I have also spent a lot of time reading the many books available on the topic of coaching.

The BASIC method has arisen as a result of synthesising everything I have learned about coaching into an approach that I have been using in my own professional coaching practice. More recently, however, I've also been using the BASIC coaching approach within family settings, as my story about Uncle Peter illustrates. I have been pleasantly surprised to discover the BASIC method works equally well at work and at home.

Using the BASIC method

The BASIC coaching method will help enable you to have really effective coaching conversations not just in formal coaching situations, but in all the everyday conversations you have at work with colleagues and members of your team. It can also help you think about the way you talk with family members, friends and even your children.

Whether you are supporting one of your colleagues to overcome a challenge, helping a team member to prioritise their tasks, or talking something through with a family member, the BASIC coaching method will give you the clarity you need to coach with confidence.

Coaching builds buy-in

As the example of my Uncle Peter reminds us, one of the greatest benefits from adopting a coaching approach to conversations is how it leaves others thinking and feeling about the future. When individuals have had the opportunity to reflect on their current situation, decide what they want to achieve and have an ownership of what can be done to move forward, they are inevitably more committed to the way ahead.

This has two key advantages:

- ◆ Because the next steps have come from the individual themselves, there is an inherently greater chance that they will actually complete them.
- ◆ There is also a much greater chance that solutions are suited to the particular situation they find themselves in.

One of the biggest risks in us just giving other people advice rather than letting them come up with solutions for themselves, is that we devise ideas which would work for us as individuals and for the situation we find ourselves in, rather than solutions for someone else and the situation they are in.

This idea applies as much to the world of work as it does to everyday life. When you are having conversations with colleagues, the more you are able to help them reflect and come up with their own ideas, the greater ownership they will have. Of course, it can be very tempting for us to suggest the answer, especially when we really want to help. As we will see shortly, there is absolutely a time and a place for giving advice and making suggestions, but for most of us, being just a little bit better at holding back from our own ideas and allowing others to come up with theirs is usually a good idea.

Staying connected with reality

Taking more of a coaching approach to conversations also means we remain more connected with the wider environment in which we are operating. This is particularly relevant to the organisational settings many of us find ourselves working in. If we stop asking questions about what is happening within our organisation, we run the risk of becoming quite disconnected from reality. By remaining curious and interested in our colleagues and their work, we can remain in touch with what is happening beyond our own individual experiences. For leaders in organisations particularly, it is clearly very important to stay connected with what is going on, both within and beyond the organisation.

Building capacity in others

Enabling colleagues, friends and family to think about the solution to a problem, or focus on what they want to achieve, will inevitably build their capacity to think for themselves and become more self-sufficient. Whether we think about this from the perspective of parents or from that of leaders within organisations, this is something we are obviously all keen to do. Over time, this approach leads to a reduced reliance upon us as the people that always know the answer or have all the knowledge and skills required.

Not top down — CONSTRUCTIVIST

What is the BASIC coaching method?

This is the point in the book where we need to be really clear about what we mean by *coaching* as the term can be interpreted very differently depending on the context. In the world of sport for example, the role of the coach might be summarised as having three key areas:

♦ To take key decisions on strategy or tactics.
♦ To advise players or athletes on how they can improve their performance.
♦ To motivate them.

In other words, for much of the time the coach is in the driving seat, using their expertise and knowledge to get results.

Personal construction of meaning.

prior knowledge — new events

16

[handwritten: knowledge is constructed, rather than INNATE or passively absorbed. Learning is an ACTIVE process.]

In a business context, a performance or executive coach will take a different approach. Their goal is much more about enabling someone to work out for themselves what they need to do and how they may go about doing it, much as I have been trying to do with my uncle.

The very best definition of this type of coaching I have come across is from Christian van Nieuwerburgh, a leading academic in the field of coaching within the education sector in the UK and beyond.

Coaching definition

A one-to-one conversation that focuses on the enhancement of learning through increasing self-awareness and a sense of personal responsibility, where the coach facilitates the self-directed learning of the coachee, through questioning, active listening and appropriate challenge in a supportive and encouraging environment.

[handwritten: Primary responsibility – create a collaborative problem solving environment]

This relatively short paragraph is nonetheless full of important concepts and ideas about what this type of coaching actually looks like in practice. It first of all recognises that coaching is all about helping others grow and develop. Secondly, at its heart is a sense of personal responsibility and ownership, drawing on a greater self-awareness and understanding both of oneself and of one's situation. Thirdly, as we have already discussed, it focuses on individuals working out for themselves their own way forward.

[handwritten: Morrison]
[handwritten: PIAGET]
[handwritten: BRUNER]
[handwritten: Learner is not an empty vessel to be filled with knowledge. DEWEY]
[handwritten: All knowledge is SOCIALLY constructed in PERSONAL VYGOTSKY]

Finally, as well as acknowledging the importance of listening really carefully, this definition also recognises that so long as a trusting relationship has been developed between the two individuals, these conversations can be challenging without feeling threatening. Because the person being coached knows that the coach's only agenda is to help, the coach can offer challenge in a way that reduces the risk of the coachee becoming defensive or disengaged.

The BASIC blend

So, is the BASIC coaching method more like the sporting example or van Nieuwerburgh's definition? The answer is that it is actually a blend of both. While a coaching approach to conversations can be a very powerful tool, there are clearly times when giving some advice is the right thing to do. If you find yourself in a situation as a coach where you are starting to feel that no matter how many questions you ask, your coachee isn't going to be able to work out what to do, of course you are going to offer some advice or show them how to do something.

Why would you deliberately withhold advice when your greater knowledge and experience means you have the answer they need?

How much time you have available is also a factor. Imagine you are at work and the fire alarm goes off. You wouldn't be recommending that individuals sit down and have a coaching conversation to discuss which door they should exit from. Often, when time is short, decisions just need to be made and advice just needs to be given. The coaching continuum opposite, heavily influenced by the thinking of Myles Downey, illustrates the range of different types of conversation we have with one another. The BASIC method of coaching spans the whole continuum, not just one end or the other.

The coaching continuum

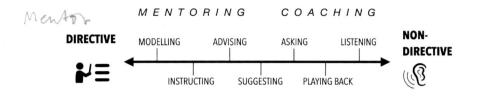

On the left of the continuum a coach is being quite directive. This is where they may be helping someone work out what to do by either modelling or instructing on a possible way forward. This is typically what mentors do when working with someone starting in a new role, giving them the benefit of their experience. In mentor mode, you are the expert, sharing your knowledge and know-how. Mentoring is similar to the sports coach example.

As we move towards the right of the continuum, a coach gradually become less directive and begins to place more and more onus on the other person to work out what they want to do and how they are going to do it. In other words, you are acting more as a coach as defined by van Nieuwerburgh. My own coaching conversations will typically be on the right of the model for the vast majority of the time, with me asking questions and helping someone to work out what they want to do.

Only offering advice

Occasionally however, I find myself in a situation where I can see someone is really struggling and from my external perspective I think I may have an idea that could help. In this situation I will offer to share the idea with the person I'm coaching.

It's important to stress, however, that this is only an offer. It's entirely up to them whether they wish to hear the idea. This approach has proved popular with my coachees and is why the definition of coaching in the BASIC method spans the whole of the coaching continuum. When I have finished sharing my idea, I will always go back into coaching mode and ask whether or not that particular idea is helpful, rather than make the assumption that it's what they need or want to do.

In my view, there is nothing more frustrating, especially when time is tight, if you can see a possible solution and feel unable to share it, but it is really important not to jump to making suggestions too soon. If you have already coached, you will know how tempting this can be, especially at the beginning. This blended approach to coaching is sometimes referred to as instructional coaching and has been brilliantly championed by Jim Knight, the founder of the Instructional Coaching Group (IGA) in the United States.

This means the BASIC definition of coaching is *wider* than van Nieuwerburgh's, allowing for modelling or the giving of advice when required.

 BASIC coaching definition

A one-to-one conversation that focuses on the enhancement of learning through increasing self-awareness and a sense of personal responsibility, where the coach facilitates the self-directed learning of the coachee, through questioning, active listening, appropriate challenge and, **when needed, practical guidance** in a supportive and encouraging environment **that leaves the coachee feeling clearer and more optimistic about the future**.

You will have noticed I have added a phrase about coachees feeling clearer and more optimistic about the future. This for me is the acid test for any coaching conversation, of any length and in any setting: does the person you are talking to leave the conversation in a better place than they were when the conversation started?

Suggesting models

Sometimes I may be having a conversation with someone and realise that I'm aware of a particular model or framework that might help them structure their thinking in some way. As with mentoring, I will always ask whether or not someone would like to explore a particular model that might help. Once I've shared the model I will move back into a coaching mode and ask whether 'there's anything here that might help' with their thinking.

Throughout this book I will share the most commonly used models that I tend to draw on in my own coaching practice. A good example would be John Kotter's change model that I will describe in Chapter 4 (Implementation). This model sets out the key steps you can use when planning how to implement a change in a way that makes it stick for the long-term, rather than just being very exciting at the start and then fizzling out. We have all experienced too many of those!

Using metacognition

When I was a headteacher, my first coach was Glyn Rawlings. Glyn was an inspirational coach and was the first person to really enable me to see the power of coaching. I found the whole process uplifting, always leaving me feeling clearer and more optimistic about the future, and I used to really look forward to our sessions.

One of the things Glyn asked me was whether or not I would find it useful for him to explain to me his thinking as he was moving through the coaching process. I was very interested in coaching and said 'yes', because I wanted to better understand the skills, techniques and approaches he was using. It was a powerful way for me to reflect on the coaching process and how I could incorporate it more into my own work; particularly in relation to how I worked with the people I line managed. That said, not everybody finds this approach useful. Some of the people I coach have told me they would prefer it just to feel like they were having a natural conversation, rather than be diverted from their own thinking by reflecting on the coaching process itself. This is why contracting with your coachee is important.

Contracting

In more formal coaching situations, when you first meet with someone and after you have spent some time just getting to know one another, it is always useful to clarify what your coaching conversations are and are not. This is often known as contracting. For me, this usually involves:

- ◆ Whether they have coached or been coached in the past.
- ◆ If they have been coached, finding out what it was that worked well in the way the other person coached them.
- ◆ Making it very clear that the coaching conversations are completely confidential and are entirely for them – I want them to understand that my only agenda is to help them.
- ◆ Agreeing some of the specifics about frequency, length and location of the coaching to enable the sessions to be most productive.
- ◆ Whether coaching off-site is possible and/or desirable.
- ◆ Discussing whether coaching remotely is a possibility.

- Ensuring we are clear on the boundaries – coaching is not therapy or counselling.
- Discussing the options around using models and/or metacognition.
- Being clear from the outset about when the coaching will end, and that a coachee can end it prematurely if it's not working for them.

Apart from giving you both real clarity about how the process will work, taking time to contract is a useful way to build rapport at the early stages of a coaching relationship.

Using a coaching approach as a line manager

Inevitably, if you are having a coaching conversation with someone who you line manage, it's not going to be the same as with someone you don't. Apart from the fact that there is an accountability within a line management relationship which is different from a pure coaching relationship, there is also the potential that as the line manager, your leadership might be part of what your coachee wants to talk about!

In an ideal world, colleagues will always have access to an external coach, or at least one who is not part of the line management chain. Having an external coach can be particularly useful when individuals are transitioning from one role to another or when taking on a new project. But with that said, using the BASIC approach in your conversations will give greater ownership clarity and optimism to a colleague, rather than it seeming that you are simply just the person who tells them what to do all the time.

I would always recommend that when two individuals start working together there is a conversation at the beginning about how your one-to-one meetings will work. As we explored earlier in this chapter, you are effectively contracting in that you are agreeing together how your conversations are going to work.

Time to reflect

To help you reflect and plan, at the end of each chapter there will be:

BASIC QUESTIONS

♦ A list of suggested questions you may want to try out in your coaching that relate to the content covered in the chapter.

BASIC REVIEW

♦ A series of questions to prompt you to reflect on the content within the chapter.

NOTES

♦ A space for you to record any high-level thoughts or intentions that have arisen from reading the chapter.

Behaviorism

Skinner

'knowledge exists independently
and outside of people'

Learner is a blank 'state' who
must be provided the experience

Learning actually occurs when
new behaviours or changes in behaviour
are acquired thro' associations
between 'stimuli' and responses

Teachers use
Behaviourism when they reward
or punish student behaviour.

BASIC QUESTIONS

✓ Have you had a coach before?
✓ What worked well that we should try to make sure we do?
✓ What do we need to avoid?
✓ If this coaching is successful, how will it help you?
✓ What are you hoping for from these sessions?
✓ Would it be useful to talk about how the sessions will work?
✓ What is the best time and place for you?
✓ How long would you like the sessions to be?
✓ How will we know if the coaching has been a success?
✓ If there is an idea or model that I think might help you, can I can share it with you?

 # BASIC REVIEW

✓ Will the BASIC coaching method be something you will try at home as well as at work?
✓ What are the advantages of using a coaching approach?
✓ How will the concept of the coaching continuum help you be an effective coach?
✓ How will you avoid the temptation to offer advice too soon?
✓ How will you use contracting as an important part of your coaching process?
✓ What is the potential for using the BASIC coaching method in your line-management meetings?
✓ Do you think using models will be a feature of your coaching?
✓ As you gain in coaching experience and confidence, do you think you may offer a metacognitive approach to your conversations?
✓ What has been most useful about this chapter for you?

NOTES

BASIC Overview

BASIC STEPS   **BASIC** QUALITIES   **BASIC** HABITS   **BASIC** FEEDBACK

This book has been written in such a way that once you have read the introduction, you can dip into any section in the order that suits you. Indeed, there is no right order to read it. The book is divided into four key parts.

Part A: BASIC **Steps** – the structure of coaching conversations.

Part B: BASIC **Qualities** – the key individual personal qualities needed.

Part C: BASIC **Habits** – the useful habits it helps for us to develop.

Part D: BASIC **Feedback** – helping your coachee to improve.

Although I have set out the content in the order shown above, I could just as easily have decided that BASIC Qualities or BASIC Habits was a good place start. The rest of this overview will give you a high-level summary of the content of each section to help you decide your reading order.

Part A: BASIC STEPS

The BASIC Steps are the five broad stages within a conversation. It is important to say right from the outset that these five steps really must be seen as a broad framework rather than a narrow set of steps that must always be followed in exactly the same order.

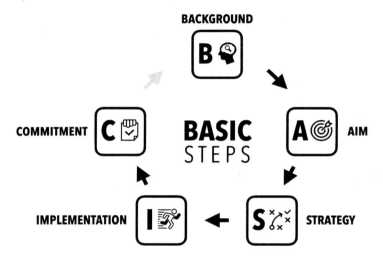

BASIC Background

♦ Understand the background to a situation.

♦ Allows the coachee to start to organise their thoughts.

♦ Opportunity to focus on the positives, not just the issues.

BASIC Aim

♦ Define the aim or goal the coachee wants to achieve.

♦ Get clarity on timeframes and what success will look like.

♦ Focus on the benefits.

BASIC Strategy

◆ Focus on the high-level options or strategy.

◆ Keep away from the detail at this stage.

◆ Really explore *all* the possibilities, not just the first ideas that emerge.

BASIC Implementation

◆ Fine tune the strategies into actions, in particular, the very next steps.

◆ Consider sketching out a rough plan of action to follow after that.

◆ Just getting someone started on their first step can be all that's needed.

BASIC Commitment

◆ Checking in on how energised your coachee is to get going.

◆ Offer positive challenge on their level of commitment if needed.

◆ Ask how they will sustain whatever they have decided to do.

A framework, not a straitjacket

While these five BASIC Steps are at the heart of how a coaching conversation can be structured, I think it is worth me reminding you again that most conversations do not need to start at the beginning and religiously work through the five steps one-by-one.

For example, you may find yourself helping a coachee explore the possible strategies or high-level options that will help them achieve their aim, and realise that it might be useful to go back to the background for a while to explore a bit more about the context. This can often help the coachee see other possible ideas. The BASIC Steps are just there as a guide to enable you to broadly structure the flow of a conversation in a way that helps people move forward.

Wider use of BASIC Steps

While this book is predominantly focused on coaching, it is perhaps also worth taking a moment to reflect on the fact that the BASIC Steps method works equally well if you are in a more directive or mentoring mode. The only difference is that you are using it yourself to structure your summary of context, aim, possible ideas and a plan of action. Taking this even further, the method can work well as a simple template for setting out a short paper, proposal or report on a particular topic. I know lots of organisations that use this approach to help them keep papers short, well-structured and easy to navigate.

Background
✓ What is our current position?
✓ Why does this matter?
Aim
✓ What is it we want to achieve?
✓ What will success look like?
Strategy
✓ How are we going to achieve it?
✓ What are the options here?
Implementation
✓ What are the key steps we need to take?
✓ Who needs to be involved?
Commitment
✓ Which is the right approach?
✓ What do we recommend?

Part B: BASIC QUALITIES

This part of the book identifies the key personal qualities that I believe are at the heart of what makes you a great person to have a conversation with!

Build Trust

- ◆ The foundation of any coaching relationship. ✓
- ◆ Builds from your rapport and sense that you care.
- ◆ Trusted for your intentions; trusted for your competence and expertise.

being HONEST

Remain Curious

- ◆ Being interested, not judgmental, changes the dynamic of conversations.
- ◆ Resisting the temptation to overlay your values on their situation.
- ◆ Being aware of when your own cognitive bias may be operating.

Been there, done that

Show Empathy   *Don't turn around / hijack*

- ◆ Showing that you understand their situation and that you care.   *the*
- ◆ Not about sympathising. ✓   *conversation*
- ◆ I understand your challenge; let's explore what you can do about it.

Stay Positive

- ◆ Focus on the future not the past. ✓
- ◆ Build from success. ✓
- ◆ Believe in your coachee's ability to effect positive change. ✓

Part C: BASIC HABITS

Ask First ✓

- ◆ Start conversations with questions.
- ◆ Resist the temptation to impose your own answers.   *YES* ✓
- ◆ Only offer advice or show how to do something if it's really necessary.   *YES* ✓

Frame Well

- ◆ Use open questions. ✓
- ◆ Challenge your coachee's thinking and perspectives.   *YES* ✓
- ◆ Trust the coaching process. ✓

Listen Hard

- Show you are listening with your body language.
- Talk less, listen more.
- Hear what's not being said.

Play Back

- Summarise what you have heard.
- Use this to prompt further thoughts.
- Let the silence do the heavy lifting.

Part D: BASIC FEEDBACK

This part of the book focuses on how to have feedback conversations that really leverage improvement and change. The focus is on how to help someone be open to feedback as well as how to ensure coachees go away with a clear idea of what they want to do and know how to do it.

Make Connections

- Start with some positive feedback; make it specific and authentic.
- Avoid the feedback sandwich.
- Use curious questions to identify potential areas for focus.

Feed Forward

- Ask first.
- Be explicit if you are moving to mentoring.
- Go back to coaching after you have mentored.

BASIC QUESTIONS

BACKGROUND
- ✓ What's on your mind?

AIM
- ✓ What do you want to achieve?

STRATEGY
- ✓ At a high level, what's the right approach to take here?

IMPLEMENTATION
- ✓ What do you need to do to make this happen?

COMMITMENT
- ✓ What are the chances you are actually going to be successful at this?

 # BASIC REVIEW

- ✓ In what order will you read the book?
- ✓ Which areas interest you the most?
- ✓ Which areas are your real strengths?
- ✓ Which may be the areas you will want to focus on?
- ✓ How easy do you think you will find working with the BASIC Steps method?
- ✓ What do you think about the idea of using the BASIC Steps method for structuring documents or presentations?
- ✓ How will you ensure the BASIC Steps method really is just a useful framework, not a straitjacket?
- ✓ What has been most useful about this chapter for you?

NOTES

1

BASIC Background

BASIC STEPS   BASIC QUALITIES   BASIC HABITS   BASIC FEEDBACK

BACKGROUND   AIM   STRATEGY   IMPLEMENTATION   COMMITMENT

This section of the book is going to focus on how to begin a coaching conversation. Getting this right is really important because it provides the platform of trust, understanding and engagement for the rest of the dialogue.

Building rapport and trust

Done well, the opening parts of a coaching conversation remind the person that they are in a safe space with someone who cares about them, is interested in their perspective, and wants them to succeed. Coaching can sometimes be that rare opportunity for an individual to explore things that are on their mind that they really can't talk to anyone else about.

Quite often this part of the conversation can be about inconsequential pleasantries that on the face of it don't contribute much to the substance of a conversation but can sometimes make a real difference to how your coachee is feeling. I recently had a conversation via Skype with someone I had not met before. The fact that I could recite the names of the five villages on the western edge of Saddleworth Moor and had visited Nora Batty's tearooms in Holmfirth (both near where he had grown up) from the days when I used to lead geography fieldtrips in the area, immediately created a connection between us that he told me afterwards he appreciated. In case you are wondering, the villages are Delph, Diggle, Uppermill, Dobcross and Greenfield!

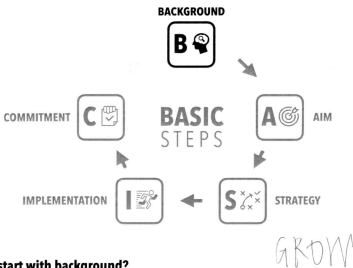

Why start with background?

GROW

Probably the most well-known coaching approach is John Whitmore's GROW model. The four stages are: **g**oal (or objective), **r**eality (the current situation), **o**ptions (what you could do) and **w**ill (what you are going to do and how committed to it you are).

When I first started coaching this was my go-to framework for structuring my coaching. Over time, however, I came to realise that most of my conversations were not starting with someone's goal or objective.

It seemed to me that when these conversations were at their most productive, we tended to spend quite a lot of time exploring the current reality of an individual's situation before we went on to then define what they wanted to achieve and how they might go about achieving it.

This is probably one of the biggest differences between the BASIC coaching method and many of the other models that are commonly used. It is my firm belief that spending time thinking about what is on someone's mind in the early stages of a conversation and then enabling them to make sense of that information, forms a very powerful building block for what comes next.

Shed your own perspective

This allows you as the coach to focus on taking the perspective of the person you are coaching, rather than imposing your own view of the world onto the conversation. By asking open questions you are able to gauge not only the facts of the situation that your coachee may be grappling with, but you can also quite quickly get a sense of the emotional energy, resilience and levels of optimism they have about the future.

As you will see in a later section of this book, deliberately looking out for these indicators of a person's state of mind can enable you to adjust your coaching approach in a way that really helps your coachee feel comfortable and able to think clearly and positively about the future.

The ladder of inference

It can be really easy for both you and your coachee to jump to conclusions about things. We will explore further the concept of what psychologists call cognitive bias in Chapter 3 (Strategy), but for now let's take a moment to examine the work of the late Chris Argyris from Harvard Business School on what he calls the ladder of inference.

The processes in the ladder often occur unconsciously and happen incredibly quickly. All the convictions we form influence us the next time we perceive a similar situation. The process continues to repeat itself and creates a vicious circle.

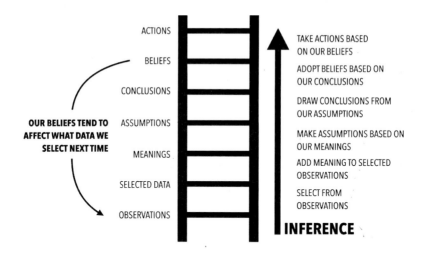

All of our conclusions reinforce our prior beliefs, which in turn influence the selection of facts. This can lead us to ignore certain facts altogether and jump to conclusions. Using the ladder of inference can be a way of helping your coachee to look at facts more objectively and not judge too soon.

Key questions you might want to ask are:

◆ Talk to me about how you reached this conclusion.
◆ I am wondering if your conclusion is actually based on facts.
◆ What do you think the other party would they say if you asked them about this?

what other party?

Create greater clarity

In his book *The Coaching Habit*, Michael Bungay Stanier identifies seven key questions which he thinks help to unlock the thinking and potential in others. Three of his questions, highlighted below, are particularly relevant when it comes to thinking about background, although I find all seven questions incredibly powerful when I am coaching.

You can hear Andy's voice!

✓ **What's on your mind?**
✓ **And what else?**
✓ **What's the real challenge here for you?**
✓ What do you want?
✓ How can I help?
✓ If you are saying yes to this, what are you saying no to?
✓ What was most useful for you?

What's on your mind?

This seems like a fairly innocuous question, but it actually allows an individual to ask themselves what it is that they want to be clearer or more optimistic about.

What is it that they're worried about? What is it that they know they need to focus on? Are they not quite sure at the moment exactly what to do?

It's very different from asking someone 'how are you?' A question like this usually garners an almost automatic response along the lines of 'I'm fine. How are you?' The other powerful element of a question like this is its neutrality. It's different from saying 'okay, what's the problem you'd like to talk about today?' which rather assumes that you're always going to be coming to these conversations with problems. Questions that contain even the slightest element of judgment within them are quite often much less effective at enabling free thinking than those that don't.

And what else?

This is probably my favourite question of all from Bungay-Stanier. Its power stems from the implicit assumption that you believe there actually is something else. But it is such an open question that your coachee really has to do all the work themselves. I have lost count of the number of times I have asked this question and my coachee has answered with something I would never have thought of – and neither would they unless challenged in this way. Rarely is someone's first answer their only answer and often it's not their best. If you think about it, this seemingly innocuous question is also very different from 'Is there anything else?' This more closed question allows for a yes or no answer and makes it very easy for your coachee to avoid thinking too hard.

What's the real challenge here for you?

This is a powerful invitation for your coachee to reflect back on everything they've just said to you and try to discover or summarise what the key issue is that might

Realize where the 'real' challenges are!

lie behind the challenge or issue that is being considered. Quite often, just taking that moment to reflect can help your coachee see something they hadn't seen before. I can remember a conversation with my Uncle Peter where I asked him this question. After thinking for a while, he realised that his challenge was not that he might get lost when he was out and about, because people always helped him. What dawned on him was the much greater risk that if he had a fall at home, he would be very vulnerable because no one would know. It prompted him to ask me to look into getting him a panic alarm he could wear round his neck.

Get to the root cause first   *ownership*   *What if they don't know?*

Giving your coachee the opportunity to decide for themselves what may lie at the heart of an issue or problem is a very powerful way of making sure that when it comes to deciding what needs to be done, you're actually focusing on the right thing. This is precisely why I think spending time on the background of a situation is so important before one starts to define what a goal or objective might look like.   *What's the real issue?*

If you don't take time together to properly consider what the real issue is in any given situation, there is a high probability that the goal you are seeking to achieve, or the strategies you think you're going to adopt to achieve them, won't really be addressing the core of the problem. In many cases it is something which is initially hidden, unseen or unrecognised which can open the way to a successful solution.

It can also be useful to keep in mind the difference between a problem and a dilemma. Problems have solutions, whereas what most of us face most of the time are dilemmas. These require us to make decisions with the aim of moving forward in a way which minimises the downsides and maximises the benefits.

Helping your coachee recognise this can be useful from the outset, particularly if they like everything to be perfect!

Using SWOT

You will no doubt already be aware of one very simple tool you can use to help a coachee review their current context. SWOT is a simple review of the internal and external factors in any given situation.

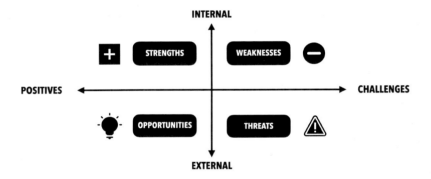

The internal elements are strengths and weaknesses that exist within a team or organisation. The external ones relate to the opportunities and threats which need to be considered.

I may not even share the actual model with some of my coachees, but simply use it as a framework in my head to help guide my questions. For others who enjoy using the actual models themselves, I might sketch it out on a piece of paper and use it as a prompt for further dialogue. As I mentioned earlier, if you do think sharing a model could be helpful, seeking agreement from the coachee is usually a good idea.

Knowing what good looks like

When you are helping your coachee reflect on the background of their situation, it can often be very helpful to ask about what information or evidence they have about what they might be aiming for. If you are coaching within an organisation, for example, does it have a set of expectations about what good looks like? If you are working in a particular sector, what does the best-practice literature suggest to your coachee they might aim for? In my own field of expertise, most educational establishments have a pretty clear view about what good teaching should look like, how the curriculum should be organised and what the approach to managing behaviour in classrooms should be. There is absolutely no point in reinventing the wheel here.

Asking about this can be a natural bridge to the next phase of the BASIC Steps method which focuses on your coachee's aim or goal.

BASIC QUESTIONS

- ✓ What's on your mind?
- ✓ What's the situation?
- ✓ What would you like to explore today?
- ✓ How did you reach this conclusion?
- ✓ Picking up from our previous meeting, update me on how you've got on?
- ✓ What are you really pleased about that you've achieved since we last met?
- ✓ Out of ten, how are you feeling about everything at the moment?
- ✓ What do you think is the real issue here?
- ✓ Just reflecting back on everything you've said, what's it left you thinking?
- ✓ Who are the key players in this situation? Tell me about them?
- ✓ What else do you think is relevant to this situation?

BASIC REVIEW

- ✓ What will you need to remember when it comes to building rapport and trust?
- ✓ Does spending time on the background before helping your coachee consider their aim make sense to you?
- ✓ How easy will you find it to shed your perspective?
- ✓ What did you think of the seven questions from Michael Bungay-Stanier?
- ✓ Why is it important to prompt your coachee to focus on the positive as well as the issue(s)?
- ✓ What is the advantage of trying to establish the root cause of an issue or challenge?
- ✓ What does SWOT stand for? How might you use this in coaching?
- ✓ How could the concept of 'knowing what good looks like' help with your coaching?
- ✓ What has been most useful about this chapter for you?

NOTES

AIM : is the WHAT of the research
OBJECTIVE : is the HOW

AIM | GOAL / OBJECTIVE : SYNONYMS?

Aim   : what you hope to achieve
Outcomes :   What steps will be taken to
                           achieve desired outcomes
goals :
                    → synonym with objective.
targets :
Objectives :   specific statements
                    that define
                    measurable
                    outcomes.

In the MOMENT

Sometimes you can't
'see'

2

BASIC Aim

Once you have helped your coachee reflect on the background and context of their situation, you should be in a position to help them gain some clarity on what it actually is that they would like to achieve: their **aim**. ※ (the what).

Taking time to map out the background really thoroughly is time very well spent. Once your coachee has expanded on what is happening at the moment and explored what some of the issues might be, potential goals will usually emerge quite naturally within the conversation. As a coach, you can really add value by helping someone define more precisely than they might otherwise do exactly what it is they want to achieve.

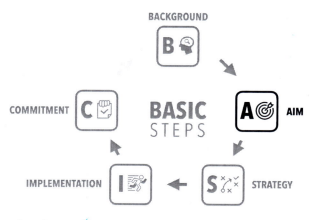

Thinking ahead

One of my coaches used to send me an email a few days before a coaching session asking me what it was that I wanted to talk about. However busy I was, it was usually useful to take a moment to reflect in advance about what was on my mind. This is probably another area to discuss and agree upon when you are contracting with a coachee. Some may prefer to just dive into the conversation at the time of the session and see where it takes them. Others may welcome the opportunity to step back from the day-to-day in advance and gather their thoughts.

Using the SMART model

You will probably be familiar with the SMART model for setting goals or targets. Whether you decide to use this model explicitly, or whether it simply guides you in the conversation you are having, it's a useful way to make sure your coachee has a well-defined goal.

(handwritten: GROWTH : coaching model)

SMART goals

S Specific
Precisely what is it you want to achieve? *(check mark)*
M Measurable
How will you know if you have achieved it? *(check mark)*
A Achievable
Are you being realistic here? *(check mark)*
R Relevant
Is this the right thing to focus on? *(check mark)*
T Timebound
When will this be completed by? *(check mark)*

John Campbell, one of the key thinkers behind the GROWTH coaching model, and who I have had the privilege of being trained by, introduced me to an *(handwritten: ✳)* alternative approach to defining goals, which I love. This deceptively simple yet powerful approach incorporates many of the features of the SMART approach but includes a couple of additional motivational elements.

(handwritten: Framing GOALS in the future.)

Framing goals in the future

(handwritten left margin: Yes this is appearing in models!)

By...
What's the timeframe?

I am/have...
What will I have achieved?

So that...
What's the benefit?

(handwritten bottom: turn over and it makes sense)

If it helps, here is an example:

- **By** the end of September;
- **I have** successfully re-organised the roles played by each member of my team;
- **So that** everybody is carrying out a role that plays to their strengths and makes us even more effective as a team.

POSITIVE PSYCHOLOGY

The emphasis on what the benefits are of achieving a particular goal draws on the growing field of positive psychology. Focusing on what can be achieved and making the assumption that it will be achieved, can change the mindset of your coachee in a very powerful way.

POSITIVE !

Clarity is motivating

At the end of coaching sessions, I often ask coachees what the most useful thing about the session has been. Quite often they will say that it has just been great to have had the time to step back from their day-to-day activities and work out what their priorities actually are. For many of us, just gaining clarity about what it actually is that we need to focus on can be liberating and motivating.

YES

When we lack that clarity, a sense of unease or foreboding can build up, making us less effective and less positive than we might otherwise be. In a sense, whether we are thinking about this at home or at work, coaching almost forces us to unravel all the issues we are grappling with and re-shape them into some clear and achievable goals.

It's or own nnn

YES ...

Revisiting the background and aim

The more I have coached, the more I have realised the benefit of coming back to an aim and either: *rehearsing ...*

◆ Using the aim to keep the discussion on track when a coachee appears to be deviating from their goal; or

◆ Spending some time re-framing the goal if subsequent discussion has revealed that what your coachee may have originally thought was their goal is actually part of a more complex or deep seated issue which needs addressing as a whole.

being able to step outside think outside the problem

I can recall one coaching conversation I had last year with a head of department who had initially thought their aim was to set up more elaborate monitoring systems to check on the work of his team. After further discussion, it turned out that this wasn't really the right goal. The vast majority of the team were performing really well and increased monitoring would have just felt to them as if they weren't trusted and would have been de-motivating. What my coachee realised was that there was one member of his team doing a poor job and that this needed addressing with the individual. The remainder of the coaching conversation was then focused on making that process a success.

Sometimes you can't see the problem!

The next part of this book will explore what it is that you as a coach can do to help others identify the right approach or strategy to achieve the aims they have set themselves.

BASIC QUESTIONS

- ✓ What does success look like on this for you?
- ✓ What do you want?
- ✓ If you did this, what do you think the outcome would be?
- ✓ By the end of our time together what do you want to have achieved?
- ✓ When we finish today what outcomes do you want to go away with?
- ✓ What is the purpose of our meeting today?
- ✓ What would good look like to you on this?
- ✓ What would make today's session a success for you?
- ✓ How would you feel if you achieved this?
- ✓ Are you sure you are aiming for the right thing here?
- ✓ What will happen if you don't achieve this

BASIC REVIEW

- ✓ Would it be useful to consider asking coachees about what they would like to talk about ahead of a session?
- ✓ Do you ensure you spend sufficient time on background and aim before thinking about what the coachee might plan to do?
- ✓ Have you thought about revisiting an aim if later in the conversation your coachee appears to be off track or you think the goal needs amending.
- ✓ Would the SMART model help you in ensuring your coachees set clear aims for themselves?
- ✓ Could the: 'By... I have... So that...' model be useful?
- ✓ How can you use the clarity that flows from a good aim to motivate your coachees?

NOTES

Aims : Something intended or desired to be obtained by one's efforts

Outcomes : end result or impact of a service, programme or intervention

Goals : A goal is an idea of the future or desired result that a person envisions, plan + commit to achieve.

* Targets :

3

BASIC Strategy

BASIC STEPS   BASIC QUALITIES   BASIC HABITS   BASIC FEEDBACK

BACKGROUND   AIM   **STRATEGY**   IMPLEMENTATION   COMMITMENT

So, your coachee has now got some clarity about what they want to achieve, which is great. But what I have learned over the last few years is that individuals at this point are usually pretty tempted to dive into the detail of what they need to do in order to achieve the objectives they've set for themselves. This is a real positive in one sense; of course we want our coachees to have an enthusiasm and a positivity about what they want to achieve. But sometimes this potential rush into action can limit the effectiveness of what they might decide to do.

In his book *Winners*, Alistair Campbell, the former director of communications for the British Prime Minister Tony Blair, talks about the importance of individuals or organisations being really clear about their **strategy** before embarking on a particular set of actions, using what he calls his OST model.

New Labour!

Objective – strategy – tactics (OST)

His main point is that once you have an objective, it is important to consider what your main *single* strategy is for achieving it. The critical point here for you as a coach is that, for any given objective, you should ideally be helping your coachee aim for only one overall strategy and then line up their tactics or actions accordingly.   *DO YOU AGREE?*

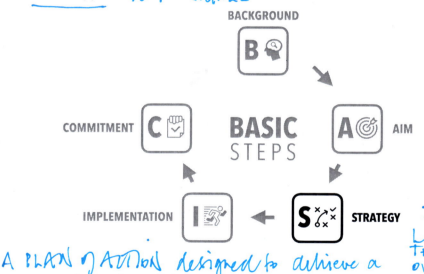

BACKGROUND

B 🔍

BASIC STEPS

COMMITMENT **C** ✓

A 🎯 AIM

IMPLEMENTATION **I** 🏃

S STRATEGY   *LONG TERM OVERALL AIM!*

A PLAN OF ACTION designed to achieve a

A good example would be at work when someone you line manage is underperforming. When you boil it down, there really are only two strategies or approaches for your coachee to take:

♦ Giving 100% support and helping to enable the person to improve.

Do you agree

or

- ◆ Having decided the person isn't really suited to – or capable of undertaking – the role, moving them on to a different role within their organisation or somewhere else.

In this case, the strategy is normally option one to start with. It's just the right thing to do: your coachee will usually want to give someone the opportunity to improve with a wide range of support. Providing high-quality coaching may very well form part of that support. But helping your coachee to be clear about whether this support is working is also important. It may be that if after a period of time things are not improving, a change of strategy is needed, and the goal needs to be moving someone on. In which case, a whole series of other actions will be needed. *which are ?*

see definition

The key point here is that once your coachee has the overall strategy or option decided, all their actions need to line up behind that strategy.

STRATEGY. *ACTIONS.*

Back to background?

I mentioned at the start of this book that while BASIC can provide a useful framework to help you structure your coaching conversations, it doesn't have to be slavishly followed. Quite often when you are exploring options for the overall strategy that someone might want to take to help them achieve their goal, it can be really useful to go back and revisit the background. After all, any potential solution needs to work for the context that your coachee is operating within. It's no good coming up with a generic solution that would work in 70% of cases if it's not going to work for your coachee. Some of the questions at the end of this chapter are designed to help individuals reflect on their context or situation, particularly when finalising their strategic approach.

Thinking fast and slow

Some of our decisions about strategy are made almost without thinking. We often rely on our intuition and experience to tell us what we need to do. The psychologist Daniel Kahneman in his book _Thinking Fast and Slow_ calls these types of decisions System 1 decisions. These are decisions we make automatically. When you turn around because there's been a loud bang behind you, for example, you are doing this instinctively. You aren't consciously thinking 'I wonder what that is; let's have a look.'

Have you made any 1/2 decisions? today

System 2 decisions, he suggests, are more rational. This is when you stop, take time to consider the situation, weigh up your options and then make your decision about what to do. Coaching conversations are an ideal place to allow someone the time and space to take decisions that are more considered and more rational.

Unconscious bias

But even then, decision-making is just not that simple. There are various factors that can stop us making logical decisions even when we are consciously trying to be rational. Psychologists have identified that there are many unconscious factors which can influence us without us even knowing. Some of the most common unconscious biases are listed below.

Any EXAMPLES ?

Anchoring

This is where you rely too heavily on a past reference or piece of information. For example, when you are thinking about what a new performance target might look like, you are too wedded to what has been achieved in the past.

Framing effect

[handwritten: An example.]

Drawing different conclusions about what to do depending on how something has been presented or pitched. This can apply to graphical information in particular. Being properly aware of how the axes on a graph are scaled is a classic example of how data can be manipulated to frame information.

Group-think

[handwritten: Any examples]

This is the tendency within a group to think the same about things, without the members of the group even realising it is happening. This is especially likely with teams where the individuals have worked together for a long time and have become friends.

[handwritten: Important WORD! Like at Rosendale / St. Leonards!]

Sunk-cost fallacy

This is where we tend to stick to a particular way of doing something because we have invested a lot of time and money into it, even though it is no longer the best way to do something.

[handwritten: Think about this one. This is IMPORTANT! YES!]

When you are coaching, being aware of both your own potential biases and those of your coachee, and bringing those out into the open, is another way your coaching can help people have self-awareness and understanding before deciding on the right approach to take.

[handwritten: shed your own perspective.]

Once you have identified a series of potential strategies, the next stage will usually be to review them all in order to decide which one is going to be the right one to adopt.

[handwritten: coaching supporting + suggesting different models?]

Pros and cons

Creating a list of *pros and cons* for each option can be a simple yet powerful way of working out which is the right approach to take. As with most decisions in life,

Yes but what about the [?] of different models

there is rarely a perfect solution. Your job as a coach is to help your coachee work out on balance which of the potential approaches is overall going to be the most effective. For every option there are likely to be downsides. When we list pros and cons, we are usually doing this in order to get a slightly clearer view of what the overall balance of the positives and negatives is for any given option we are considering.

BEHAVIOURISM V. CONSTRUCTIVISM.

Binary decision-making matrix

If your coachee finds themselves with a choice between just two options, it may be useful to consider using the binary decision-making matrix. This diagnostic tool was actually invented during a coaching conversation a few years ago when someone was faced with a dilemma about whether to make a particular change or not. Rather than just considering the pros and cons, this technique allows a more subtle interrogation of the advantages and disadvantages of the two options on the table.

You will see from the diagram below that rather than having two columns representing pros and cons, there are now four domains. When I am using this with coachees, the first stage is to ask them to list all the things they can think of in each of the four domains. I then ask them to consider (usually using a scale of one to five) how big an issue each of the points they have listed actually is. Just because one domain has a long list of items, doesn't necessarily mean that it has a greater weight. It depends on the relative importance of each of the points listed.

ANY EXAMPLES] This ANY illustration?

Once each listed item has been given a value from one to five, I then ask them to add up the total score in each of the four quadrants. The final stage is then to add

[illustrative?]

together the scores for the diagonal boxes. The top left and bottom right add up to give you a number in favour of no change. The other two add up to give you a value for making the change.

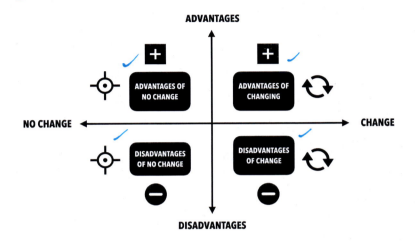

Whether you are using a pros and cons technique, the binary decision-making matrix or some other way of helping your coachee think rationally and logically about their options, there is a risk that decisions are brought down to the bare numbers. While this can be enormously helpful, there is also an important place for what your coachee may be intuitively thinking.

It's one way of quantifying things.

Logic versus intuition

Going back to Kahneman's model, while it is of course important to take a hard, rational look at the situation, our intuition is something we shouldn't ignore. So, in the final stages of deciding upon the right strategic approach, helping your coachee weigh up the rational arguments alongside what their gut feeling is telling them can also be a useful process to undertake. When I reflect back over the last few years, the majority of the coaching conversations I've had have been about people in one way or another, which is where intuition comes in. People do not always think or behave rationally, so including intuition as part of any decision-making process is useful.

HUMAN KIND

Summarise the strategy

Once a clear strategy appears to have emerged, it's often quite useful to ask the person you are coaching to play back in a single sentence or two what they think sums up the strategy they have arrived at. This can often tease out any unresolved questions, as well as giving your coachee a sense of confidence and motivation for taking the next steps.

Once they have clearly defined their overall strategic approach, the next part of the book will explore how you can help your coachee draw up a powerful plan of action.

→ Strategy — for
NEXT PHASE

Have a focus !
Be disciplined
Study ..

Don't just 'drift'

BASIC QUESTIONS

- ✓ What do you think might work in this situation?
- ✓ Have you been in a similar situation before and if so, what did you do that worked?
- ✓ What else could you do?
- ✓ Which of these options do you think is most likely to work?
- ✓ What's the right thing to do for your team or for the people that are involved in this?
- ✓ What's your gut feeling about this?
- ✓ How would you know if this has been successful?
- ✓ How can we weigh up the pros and cons of each of these options?
- ✓ Would it be useful to sit down and analyse how likely each of these options is to be successful?
- ✓ Can you summarise the strategy or overall approach you have decided upon?

 # BASIC REVIEW

- ✓ How might the Objective - Strategy - Tactics model be useful in your coaching to ensure your coachee thinks about their overall strategy before diving into actions?
- ✓ How will you know when it might be useful to revisit *background* when your coachee is exploring their options?
- ✓ How could you incorporate the idea of pros and cons or the binary decision-making matrix into your coaching?
- ✓ What do you think is the right balance between logic and intuition when it comes to your coachee deciding on a strategic approach?
- ✓ What has been most useful about this chapter for you?

NOTES

4

BASIC Implementation

BASIC STEPS   BASIC QUALITIES   BASIC HABITS   BASIC FEEDBACK

BACKGROUND   AIM   STRATEGY   **IMPLEMENTATION**   COMMITMENT

Getting to this point is all very well, but in the end what matters is that something changes for the better for your coachee. We are now at the stage of **implementation** and in particular a focus on what the very first steps need to be for your coachee to move forward with confidence.

Very often just getting started on something is the most important step to achieving success.

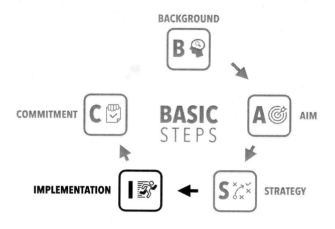

The implementation continuum

I tend to think of implementation as existing along another coaching continuum. This time, at one end of the continuum may just be a short list of actions, which is all that is needed for someone to achieve their goal or at least get started. For other coaching conversations you may well find that the goal you have been discussing requires a much more detailed action plan for implementation to be successful.

One of the things it's important to judge within a coaching conversation is to what extent this plan needs to be created within the conversation itself. For example, if someone wants to embark on an ambitious new project at work it may well be that in your coaching conversation it's absolutely fine for your outcome to be that they have decided that within the next seven days they will have drawn up a detailed action plan that lists all the key milestones that need to be put in place. This can apply equally as much at home, for example when to deciding to book a holiday or move house.

First steps matter

It may sometimes feel like a small thing, but helping someone identify exactly when they're going to take the first step can really help them begin to make progress towards their goal. For example, the outcome of your coaching conversation may be that your coachee needs to have a difficult conversation with someone in their family or at work which they've been putting off for a while. Talking through with them when the very best time would be to have this conversation could really help ensure they actually take that difficult first step. Otherwise, what typically happens is that the conversation gets put off and put off. The risk of procrastination can never be fully eliminated, but by helping someone decide on a particular time and place for when the conversation will happen, you increase the chances of it actually taking place.

Planning substantial change

For many coaching conversations, talking through the first few steps will be sufficient, but you may find yourself in a situation where you have a bit more time and where your coachee would value the opportunity to talk through in more detail the specific steps they need to take to see a project through to completion. I have found that using a model to think about what the various elements of such a plan might look like can be useful.

There are a number of well-known change management models you can use: my favourite is probably John Kotter's *Eight Steps of Change* model which I have adapted below for a coaching context.

Create the right conditions

This first stage is often the one I find coachees tend to want to jump past, instead moving straight into action. Helping them to pause and think about how they can win hearts and minds can often be time well spent. In particular, being clear about the *why* for any particular change or project pays huge dividends. If people understand why a change is necessary, we're usually half-way there. Helping your coachee identify a small group of people to work with to come up with ideas can also be a useful way to create buy-in, especially if they include someone who is more cynical. Better to have them 'inside the tent' than being critical from afar.

Get things started

Once you have created a clear vision it's time to launch or sell your idea. Rarely is this best done via email! Whether the project is home or work based, instigating it face to face is usually the best way of kicking it off. You also need to help your coachee make sure that everything is in place for the change to be a success and try, if you can, to help them identify some 'quick wins' such as saving people time or making something easier to do. This means people start to feel positive about the change.

Deliver great results
Finally, it's important to make sure that changes are embedded. This includes tackling your laggards, typically the 15% in any organisation who are the last people to adopt a new idea or change. Helping your coachee work out who these people are – and how they're going to overcome any resistance they might present – can be time very well spent. The sorts of situations where I have shared Kotter's model in a coaching session have been where the coachee is launching a new initiative or wants to change the way a system or process works in their team or organisation.

Carry out a pre-mortem

The last idea I'd like to share with you when it comes to thinking about implementation is what is known as the pre-mortem. You're probably very familiar with the post-mortem: it's all about finding the answer to the question; 'Why did they die?'

Well, the pre-mortem is about prompting your coachee to identify in advance what the biggest risks are to a change or project being successful. In other words, asking the question along the lines of; 'If your plan to achieve your goal were to fail, what's the most likely reason for this?' Sometimes, this can be as simple as speaking to people in the wrong order! Challenging your coachee to think through not only what needs to be done, but also the right order to do things can be really helpful. For most projects or plans, working out the potential pitfalls in advance and doing something about these before you start usually takes a lot less time than trying to fix problems after they have occurred. As a coach, creating the time and space for your coachee to think about issues like this can really add value to planning and decision-making at home or at work.

A great model for thinking about why something might not work out is the *Dimensions of Change* model from Knoster, Thousand and Villa. It suggests there are five key elements which are necessary for something to be implemented well. If one element is missing, there is a consequence. I am sure you can think of your own examples using the template below to guide you.

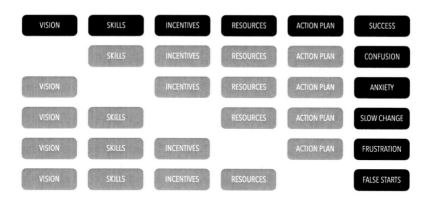

VISION	SKILLS	INCENTIVES	RESOURCES	ACTION PLAN	SUCCESS
	SKILLS	INCENTIVES	RESOURCES	ACTION PLAN	CONFUSION
VISION		INCENTIVES	RESOURCES	ACTION PLAN	ANXIETY
VISION	SKILLS		RESOURCES	ACTION PLAN	SLOW CHANGE
VISION	SKILLS	INCENTIVES		ACTION PLAN	FRUSTRATION
VISION	SKILLS	INCENTIVES	RESOURCES		FALSE STARTS

I can think of numerous examples where I have been holding this model in my head and used it to frame particular questions, depending on what I have heard and not heard. Where I wasn't sure I had much from a coachee about how she was ensuring staff understood why the change – a new information system – was necessary I asked: 'How confident are you that your staff will know why this new system is needed?' This prompted a whole line of thinking and planning about winning hearts and minds. In this case, the pre-mortem question resulted in the coachee saying the biggest risk was that the change was rushed through. As a result, she decided to slow the implementation process to ensure a sustainable outcome.

In another example where I was curious about whether a coachee who was launching a new approach to communicating with customers had really seen the need for a detailed plan, I kept asking him 'what else' needed to be in the plan. Before we knew it, another six key steps had been added.

The final part of the implementation step will usually naturally transition into the commitment phase of the conversation.

BASIC QUESTIONS

- ✓ What do you think you need to do first?
- ✓ What do you need to consider before doing anything else?
- ✓ What are the obstacles here that you need to overcome?
- ✓ Bearing in mind your overall strategy, what do you need to actually do?
- ✓ When is the best time to do this?
- ✓ What else do you need to do?
- ✓ Who else needs to be kept in the loop on this?
- ✓ What can I do to help?
- ✓ Do you need to plan out the whole thing?
- ✓ Who else is involved in this?
- ✓ If this doesn't work, what might be the main reason for its failure?

BASIC REVIEW

- ✓ How will the idea of the implementation continuum help you in how you coach in this phase of a conversation?
- ✓ How do you think John Kotter's change model might be useful to help you make sure your coachees are thinking through how to implement a change?
- ✓ What do you think of the idea of using the concept of a pre-mortem to identify in advance why a plan may fail?
- ✓ How can Knoster, Thousand and Villa's *Dimensions of Change* model help with this?
- ✓ What has been the most useful part of this chapter for you?

NOTES

5

BASIC Commitment

BASIC STEPS   BASIC QUALITIES   BASIC HABITS   BASIC FEEDBACK

BACKGROUND   AIM   STRATEGY   IMPLEMENTATION   **COMMITMENT**

The final chapter in this part of the book is pretty short. For some coaching conversations, it may not even be necessary, particularly if you can see your coachee is raring to get started on their first step.

Gaining **commitment** is all about you making sure that you have done all you can to ensure that your coachee has the greatest chance possible of achieving their goal.

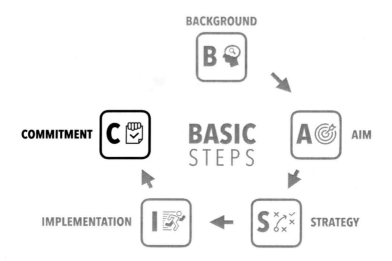

Gauging commitment

One really useful way of doing this can be to ask them to consider what they think the chances are, out of ten, that they will do what they have decided to do. Experience has taught me that if that answer is seven or less, there is a good chance they may well not be as successful as they are hoping.

Whatever the answer they give to this question, if it is anything less than a ten, it is always useful to ask what they can do to get the number up. If they say a six, I might respond with something like: 'OK, so it's not a four or a five, which is good! How could you get this up to an eight, do you think?'

This technique of using a score out of ten is known as *scaling* and can be a really useful way to gauge commitment as well as provide helpful clarity and self-awareness for your coachee.

Offering some tough love

If your commitment to your coachee is to give them 100% support, this doesn't always mean that you can't challenge them. In fact, if we really care about someone, it can sometimes mean we absolutely need to deliver a difficult message.

If we think about what makes a great parent, it isn't backing down every time your child seems to get upset about something (although there are times when that may be the right thing to do). The very best parents know that they sometimes have to offer some tough love. I think the same is true in coaching when it comes to the issue of commitment. If your coachee has decided on a particular course of action and you don't think they will follow through on it, you owe it to them to say so. At that point, they can either raise their commitment or recalibrate their goal into something that is more realistic that they can commit to with confidence.

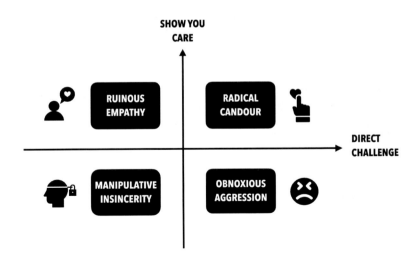

In her book *Radical Candour*, Kim Scott expands on this concept. Fundamental to her approach is the notion that challenging conversations need to be underpinned by trust and care as well as honesty. The other person knows you care about them and want them to do well. Radical candour is that powerful combination of challenging directly while showing you care about the individual.

This avoids several risks:

- Ruinous empathy: this is often rooted in not wanting to upset people in the false belief that it will build effective relationships. In the end, people lose trust if all they ever get is positive feedback and no areas for development or challenge.
- Obnoxious aggression: when you criticise without taking a moment to show the person that you care. Your approach will feel very unkind to the recipient.
- Manipulative insincerity: when you don't care enough about the person to be straight with them and are only concerned with praising just to be liked or gain some sort of advantage.

Although in her book Kim Scott is primarily thinking of leaders within organisations, it seems to me that there are lessons here for us as coaches too. If our role is to truly support someone to achieve their goals, it may be that we are the only person who can be honest with them about something. The concept is certainly useful in family life too.

When I think of some of my conversations with Uncle Peter, there have been times when it has felt like I've been pretty tough on him precisely because I love him and care about him. His resilience and determination are wonderful features of his personality and are probably the reason why he is still able to live independently. But there are times when he needs my direct challenge to see that there are certain things that are just too risky for him to do now. I was recently concerned that when he went out for his daily walk he was getting lost and on a number of occasions had to be helped home by very kind members of the public. I asked him: 'What might have happened if no one had been there to help?' He said it would have been fine and he would have found his way home eventually.

So, I asked him a more leading question: 'How busy is the road nearby and what could have happened if it had got dark before you had got safely home, particularly given your poor vision, Peter?' He was still saying he would manage. So, I replied: 'Peter, I don't think you are being honest with yourself about this. I know you want to keep your independence and I so admire this about you, but you need to face facts: you can't go on forever taking risks like this.' I let the *silence do the heavy lifting* and he eventually said that he would work out a shorter route that avoided going near the busy road.

Part of the reason I am able to have a conversation like this with my uncle is because he trusts me. In the next chapter, the first of four chapters on BASIC Habits, we will examine how you can build trust with your coachees.

BASIC QUESTIONS

- ✓ What is your commitment to doing this?
- ✓ Out of ten, what is the likelihood that what you have decided to do will actually happen?
- ✓ What could you do to make this score out of ten higher?
- ✓ Who or what can help you stick to what you have decided?
- ✓ What could stop you achieving this?
- ✓ What can do about it?
- ✓ Who can help you with this?
- ✓ I am wondering if you are really being honest with yourself about this?
- ✓ I'm saying this because I want you to succeed, but are you sure you'll actually do this?
- ✓ Can you summarise in a sentence how you are going to make sure this gets done?
- ✓ When exactly are you taking the first step on this?

 # BASIC REVIEW

- ✓ Why does it matter that as a coach you check for your coachees commitment?
- ✓ In what circumstances might this not be necessary?
- ✓ To what extent do you think Kim Scott's concept of Radical Candour is useful in a coaching context?
- ✓ Looking at the four quadrants, where do you think you tend to operate most naturally?
- ✓ What might you want to change about this?
- ✓ What has been most useful about this chapter for you?

NOTES

6

Build Trust

BASIC STEPS   **BASIC QUALITIES**   BASIC HABITS   BASIC FEEDBACK

BUILD TRUST   REMAIN CURIOUS   SHOW EMPATHY   STAY POSITIVE

When I was a headteacher, I had the privilege of working with architects and builders to design a brand-new secondary school. At the end of the tender process we ended up appointing a French company called Bouygues to build our school. One of the reasons we chose this company – apart from the price and the quality of their designs – was because we felt we would really be able to partner with the organisation to deliver an amazing school. It was therefore no surprise for me to see that the company's corporate strap line was 'The first thing we build is trust'.

Essentially, that is what they had done with us as potential clients and it had worked.

In this section of the book we're going to examine the personal qualities that coaches at their best are able to demonstrate. The first, **building trust**, is at the heart of any good relationship, and relationships, of course, form the bedrock for successful coaching conversations, whether at home or at work.

Why as a coach is it important to build trust? From all the reading I have done on the subject, I always return to Stephen Covey and his excellent work *The Speed of Trust* which is listed in my recommended reads at the end of this book.

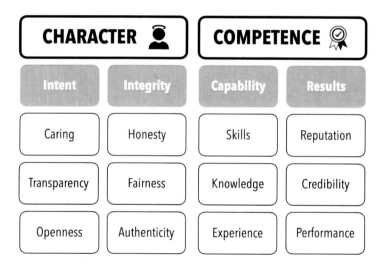

Stephen Covey breaks down the reasons why we are trusted into two key areas: our character and our competence. Let's explore these for a moment. Imagine a situation where you are leading an expedition to the North Pole and one of the team members approaches you the night before the final push to the Pole and says to you 'Do you think I should go tomorrow? Am I good enough?'

If your answer is 'Yes, you're going to be fine' it's likely that the team member will, consciously or unconsciously, be asking themselves two fundamental questions:

♦ Are you being honest with me?
♦ Do you know what you are doing?

Character

The first question is whether or not you are being straight with them. Are you saying what you really think, or just what you think they want to hear? In other words, are you being honest, transparent and open? All these qualities are features of your *character*.

Competence

Let's assume, however, that when you say 'Yes, you're going to be fine' that you really mean it. There is nonetheless another nagging question going through their mind: do you know what you are talking about? Have you brought people like them back from the North Pole alive? In other words, people trust you not just because you're decent and honest and have good intent.

They also trust you because they believe you know what you're doing and have the necessary skills and expertise to successfully execute whatever it is you're embarking on. They trust your *competence*.

So, what are the implications for you as a coach? In a nutshell, you need to build trust as fast as you can, bearing in mind both these elements.

Signalling your intent

One way to build trust quickly is to *signal your intent*. An obvious opportunity to do this is in the initial contracting conversation you have at the start of a coaching relationship. But there are opportunities at the beginning of every coaching conversation, as well as during them, when you can build rapport and signal your intent. So, what do I mean by signalling intent?

It basically means that you explain to your coachee in advance what they can expect from you in terms of your behaviours and the way in which you will be working with them. It is effectively what should happen anyway in a good contracting conversation. For example, you will be (i) stressing the importance of confidentiality; (ii) reminding them that the agenda will be set by them as the coachee, not by you; and (iii) explaining that your job is to listen, try to understand their context, and help them work out their own way forward.

You then obviously need to make sure that you deliver on those promises. What is powerful about signalling these behaviours *in advance* is that your coachee is more likely to notice that you're doing what you said you were going to do than if you hadn't signalled your intent in the first place.

It sounds like a small point, but if someone is thinking that you have clearly kept to the confidentiality that you talked about last time or that you have definitely enabled them to find their own way forward, this will build trust more quickly than if you hadn't made it explicit. Without this signalling, although the coachee may appreciate those behaviours and personal qualities you are exhibiting, it will take them longer to trust you.

Believe in your coachee

Your coaching relationships are not just about your coachee trusting you, although this is obviously vital. It is also important for you to trust in the coaching process and in your coachee's ability to own and effect positive change for themselves. This isn't always easy. In Chapter 8 (Show Empathy) we will explore the difference between showing sympathy and showing empathy. In the latter, you are able to appreciate your coachee's perspective but also keep a positive belief that they can do something about the issue or challenge they face, rather than succumb to self-pity or lose confidence. Continuing to trust and believe in your coachee's character and competence can make a real difference to how they feel, and therefore to the overall effectiveness of your coaching.

I can recall a coaching session with someone who ran a large fundraising department within a well-known charity. He was facing all sorts of challenges in hitting his income generation targets for the year and had pretty much given up on being able to do anything about it. It would have been easy for me to have colluded in his defeatism, but I trusted in both him and the coaching process itself. I helped him to explore similar situations he had faced before and been successful in overcoming.

I had no idea such situations existed, but I had to trust they would. By the end of the conversation he had regained his self-belief, set himself short-, medium- and long-term goals and was feeling far clearer and more optimistic about the future. By the way, although he didn't quite hit the revenue target he was aiming for, he was only just below it and his line manager was delighted, given all the unforeseen issues he had faced along the way.

One great way to trust the coaching process is to keep an open mind as a coach. Remaining curious and interested is a fundamental coaching quality and the subject of the next BASIC chapter.

BASIC QUESTIONS

- ✓ Can you say a bit more about that?
- ✓ Tell me why this matters to you?
- ✓ How can I help you with this?
- ✓ Can I share a model that might help with this?
- ✓ I have had a thought about this; would you like to hear it?
- ✓ When you have been in a situation like this before, what did you do that worked?
- ✓ What is working well for you in the way our conversations are happening?
- ✓ What can I do differently to make our conversation even better for you?
- ✓ Sounds like you have a plan here; what's your first step?

 # BASIC REVIEW

- ✓ How is building trust important when it comes to forming a good relationship with your coachees?
- ✓ What do you think of Stephen Covey's model for building trust?
- ✓ How do you build trust be increasing your coachee's awareness of your integrity and character?
- ✓ How can you show your coachee that you are competent and know what you are doing without appearing arrogant?
- ✓ How well do you just trust the BASIC coaching method to just work, without you having to do all the thinking?
- ✓ How do you signal to your coachees that you believe in them?

NOTES

7

Remain Curious

BASIC STEPS   **BASIC QUALITIES**   BASIC HABITS   BASIC FEEDBACK

BUILD TRUST   **REMAIN CURIOUS**   SHOW EMPATHY   STAY POSITIVE

Thinking back to the phone calls with my Uncle Peter, I am reminded of the difference between the successful and the less successful conversations we have. When my uncle feels that I really want to understand what he thinks and what he needs, things tend to move along quite smoothly. In the conversations that don't go so well, he tends to get quite defensive and not really engage with the suggestions or offers of help I am making. Reflecting on the successful conversations, the key difference is not just that I am asking more and talking less. It's also that my whole demeanour is much more one of curiosity and interest, rather than one where I make him feel that in some way I am judging him. Of course, nothing could be further from the truth, but I strongly suspect that's how I can sometimes make him feel.

I can remember when we were discussing how the two of us could visit my father in Edinburgh while he was still alive. For me, the obvious way to do this would be to fly up from Gatwick. The airport transfers at either end would be about 30 minutes, and helping Peter navigate the airports would be relatively easy. There was just one small problem: my Uncle Peter didn't have a driving licence or a passport. In talking this through, in hindsight, we had a very clear aim: get to Edinburgh and visit my dad, but I had come to the conversation with a pre-determined strategy of how to achieve it: to fly. Rather than explore the other potential options like getting the train, I felt myself getting frustrated with Uncle Peter. I wasn't really interested in understanding his perspective. Fortunately, I realised what was happening and was able to manage my own emotions in a way that meant my uncle felt I was interested in his perspective rather than just disappointed in him. As we discussed this more, I came to see that the train option had lots of advantages. I also regained some perspective. After all, the whole point of my involvement in this was to reunite two brothers and make them both happy. Doing this in a way that Peter wasn't happy with rather missed the point. While this recollection isn't really an example of a coaching conversation as such, I mention it because it does illustrate quite well how one's approach or demeanour in any conversation can fundamentally change how it feels for the other person.

Remain curious and interested

I don't believe any coach sets out to make their coachee feel judged, but it can be very easy to appear judgmental without actually realising. When you are at your best as a coach, it's almost as if you need to leave your own world behind and somehow enter your coachee's, seeing everything from their perspective. When we do this, it can really change the dynamic of a conversation because your coachee immediately feels more able to say what they really think without the fear that in some way you will think any less of them. Being genuinely curious and interested in what they think can create a powerful and empowering dynamic within your conversations.

There are clearly links between the personal qualities of remaining curious and building trust. If your coachee thinks you only have their own interests at heart and aren't trying to overlay your own views or perspectives, the trust between you will grow.

Hidden signals

Without us realising, we all send one another signals about how and what we are thinking and feeling, and we also sub-consciously pick up these signals. Our body language and tone of voice add powerfully to our choice of words, indeed, some research has indicated that in certain situations we communicate far more through these non-verbal channels than through what we actually say. Having said that, I am going to be honest and say that I have an issue with the emphasis that some coaching books place on the importance of coaches thinking about their body language in what feels to me to be a rather mechanistic and potentially patronising way. Of course, this whole area is really important and as coaches we should do our best to convey the right non-verbal messages. But my own view is that if we allow the right personal qualities and personal habits to come to the forefront, the body language and tone of the conversation will to a large extent take care of itself.

I am not saying you shouldn't pay attention to whether your body posture is open and inviting, whether you are smiling enough or whether you are remembering to nod in all the right places. But in the end, to over-think this feels rather artificial and runs the risk of reducing, not increasing your coachee's trust in you.

Don't ask why

As I mentioned earlier, we can often appear judgmental as coaches even when we don't intend to. We may genuinely be interested in understanding a particular perspective but just the way that we ask a question can make it feel quite judgmental. In particular, starting any question with the word *why* brings with it a high probability that someone will feel you're judging them. Take a question like 'Why did you decide to do that?' It may seem a fairly innocuous thing to ask and your intention is simply to find out something, but to your coachee it may well feel like a challenge; that in some way you don't think they should have decided to do what they did.

A much better way might be to ask something like 'What was it about the situation that meant you decided to take that decision?' The difference here is that the second question has within it an implication that the decision was thoughtful and context-related, whereas the first runs a much greater risk of producing a more defensive response.

Use neutral and open questions

The other thing that can really help your coachee to think deeply and for themselves is to use more open questions. Let's imagine for a moment that you're in the *background* part of a conversation and are curious to understand why someone your coachee has mentioned – let's call him John – might be behaving in the way that he is.

If you were to say: 'I'm interested in what you think might explain why John is behaving like this' you will really allow your coachee to think without any sense of you imposing your own view or limiting their thought process in any way. Contrast this with asking: 'Do you think John is upset with you in some way?' This question not only runs the risk of sending your coachee down a train of thought that may be nothing to do with the reason for John's behaviour, it also implies you think your coachee may have done something to upset John, which could feel quite judgmental and may be completely incorrect.

Remembering to ask open questions can be difficult because as a coach, while we may know that it's our job to enable our coachees to come up with perspectives and solutions for themselves, it can be hard to resist the temptation to offer suggestions simply by asking very leading questions.

Be patient

When I first started coaching, I found this whole area very tricky. Over time, however, as I've seen the power of using open questions, I have found it much easier to avoid falling into the trap of limiting a coachee's thought process by asking questions that lead them towards what I think is the answer or solution.

The other thing that has really helped me with this has just been to remind myself at the start of any coaching conversations to keep interested and curious. This almost automatically means you help your coachee to discover what *they think* rather than imposing *your own* views. This takes time but with focus and practice, you will see how powerful remaining curious can be.

The third personal quality we will explore in this section of the book is very much linked to this and is the subject of our next chapter: how can we show empathy?

BASIC QUESTIONS

- ✓ Out of ten, how are you feeling about your job today?
- ✓ What are you most pleased about since we last spoke?
- ✓ How does this make you feel?
- ✓ What really matters to you about this?
- ✓ I'm interested in this. What did you do?
- ✓ How did they react?
- ✓ That must have been difficult to hear. How did you respond?
- ✓ What do you think about this now?
- ✓ I'd be fascinated to know more about this. What happened next?
- ✓ What was it about the situation that prompted this course of action?

BASIC REVIEW

- ✓ How does remaining interested and curious rather than judgmental help you to be a better coach?
- ✓ How does avoiding starting your questions with 'why' help to reduce the risk that your coachee thinks you are judging them?
- ✓ How easy do you find it to ask positive, open and neutral questions?
- ✓ Do you ask follow-up questions that show you are genuinely interested in your coachee's perspective rather than imposing yours?
- ✓ Developing a genuinely curious demeanour can take time. How easy will this be for you?
- ✓ What has been most useful about this chapter for you?

NOTES

8

Show Empathy

BASIC STEPS **BASIC QUALITIES** BASIC HABITS BASIC FEEDBACK

BUILD TRUST REMAIN CURIOUS **SHOW EMPATHY** STAY POSITIVE

Recent research in the field of neuroscience means we know that 98% of us have the ability to empathise actually wired into our brains. The other 2% by the way are psychopaths, their inability to show empathy is pretty much what defines their condition. But just because the ability to empathise is there in most of us, it doesn't necessarily mean we always make the most of it. In this chapter we will explore what we mean by empathy and how it can help us be even better coaches.

First of all, let's examine the link between empathy and emotional intelligence. There are a number of different theoretical models that exist in relation to the concept of emotional intelligence, and empathy plays a key role in all of them. Having an awareness of someone else's perspective is fundamental in determining the quality of relationships we are able to build.

Emotional intelligence

One of the most well-known coaching models was proposed by Daniel Goleman in his excellent book *Emotional intelligence - why it can matter more than IQ*. Each element of his model has a relevance for us when it comes to coaching.

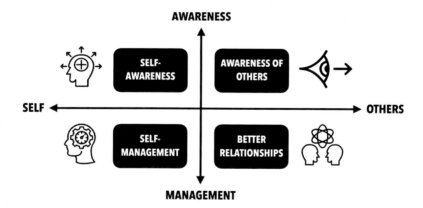

Self-awareness

Goleman has identified four key domains for emotional intelligence (EQ). He argues that our EQ begins with our own self-awareness: our ability to recognise emotions within ourselves. For example, when you are starting to feel frustrated with your coachee for some reason, maybe because they seem too reluctant to accept that something needs to change, instead of allowing this to show, a good coach will identify the emotion and use this self-awareness to then manage their response. With my Uncle Peter, for example, I can think of a number of occasions when I didn't feel he was facing up to the fact that he was getting older and would need to make adjustments. I really had to bite my tongue to prevent myself showing that frustration, as I had learned to my cost that to do so would simply make him even more entrenched in his position.

Self-management
So, it follows that our ability to manage emotions is therefore predicated on our ability to recognise them in the first place. But just identifying an emotion is not enough on its own, you need to be able to manage that emotion in a way that is productive within your coaching conversations. This isn't always easy and when I think about my own EQ, this is the area I struggle with the most. I know that I am feeling frustrated and want to offer suggestions, for example, but that doesn't make it any easier when it comes to how I actually respond. The strategy I have been working on over the last few years which has helped me manage my own emotions more effectively has been to predict in advance of a conversation any emotional responses I think I may have. This means I am more *ready for them* when they happen and can therefore manage them just that little bit more effectively. With my uncle, I remind myself before a call that he tends to need time and space before seeing the full picture and that I need to allow him that leeway.

Awareness of others
Picking up signals from others by noticing: (i) what they say, (ii) their tone of voice and (iii) their body language is at the heart of being able to empathise with a coachee. Some of us are naturally better at this than others, but the evidence

suggests that all of us can get better. It just takes a deliberate and sustained focus on really trying to notice what your coachee is saying or doing.

Better relationships
Goleman argues that better relationships are created as a result of the powerful combination of better self-management *and* self-awareness. When we are in touch with our emotions, are able to channel them effectively and can empathise with our coachee, our relationship will strengthen.

Getting too close

One of the challenges that can come with trying to enter our coachee's world is that we can lose ourselves in their issues and find ourselves sympathising with their situation. We may find ourselves wanting to say things like: 'That must be really difficult. You must feel awful. At least you...' I'll come back to how we sometimes use 'at least' in a moment. Of course, this is a very natural response. For people we care about, whether at work or at home, we want them to know that they matter to us and that we understand how difficult things are for them. While sympathy is a socially acceptable gesture, it isn't that helpful when it comes to coaching. Empathy is a far more useful form of expression.

Empathy not sympathy

So, what's the difference between sympathy and empathy? In this area the work of Brené Brown has been most influential in my thinking. Sympathy, while highly valued in our culture, can actually be very disempowering in certain situations. At its most corrosive, the sympathetic perspective can make your coachee feel like what you are subconsciously saying is effectively 'Poor you. I am sorry that you have this problem that can't really be fixed'. While this may be nowhere near what you actually mean to construe, it might appear so from your coachee's perspective. Expressing sympathy this way can accentuate a *victim* state of mind and is less likely to empower someone to resolve a situation. All you are doing is reinforcing the scale of an issue or problem without offering any hope.

For example, if someone has an issue with a work colleague they are finding it difficult to get along with and who may even be bullying them, the sympathetic response would be to acknowledge the issue and how it must be really difficult, but then go on to try and lift their spirits by reminding them that *at least* there are lots of other colleagues they get on with. There is an apparent acceptance that nothing can be done about the difficult colleague and an attempt to look on the bright side with the *at least* statement.

As a coach, you are effectively colluding with your coachee in their negativity, rather than acknowledging the problem but then challenging them to think about what can be done to address it. You will see the overlap here with Kim Scott's concept of *radical candour* we explored in Chapter 5 (BASIC Commitment).

When you come from an empathetic perspective, you understand what your coachee is feeling, and show that you understand, but you don't accept that nothing can be done. Instead, you view them as capable of working through the issue at hand. To be empathetic to someone who has a problem or issue, you might say something like: 'I sense that this is difficult. What would help the situation?'

Of course, there are times when showing pure sympathy is absolutely the right approach. If someone has suffered a huge personal loss, trying to see the positive side of that is both insulting and unhelpful. So too is trying to make them feel better with any statements that might begin with *at least*...

The drama triangle

Above all, resist the temptation feel it is your job to *rescue* your coachee. Empathy is about showing understanding; being able to place yourself in their shoes while giving them the responsibility for finding the way forward. It's why the coaching approach to conversations is so powerful. As tempting as it can sometimes be to play the rescuer when your coachee is playing the victim, manage that emotion by reminding yourself that using a coaching approach is the way to give them the opportunity to find the strength they need for themselves. This links to what is sometimes called the drama triangle in which there are three protagonists.

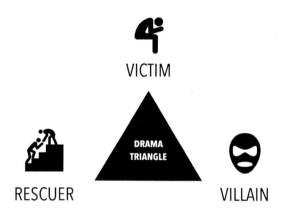

The victim

Their basic position is *poor me*. I am powerless and need to be helped or rescued. I don't really want to own my situation.

The rescuer

They feel guilty if they don't go and help someone who is in difficulty, but their help can breed a dependency which isn't usually helpful. Rescuers themselves can also become dependent on the need to rescue, as it can deflect them from thinking about their own anxieties or issues.

The persecutor or villain

The perspective of the victim is that *it's all someone else's fault*. That the villain is controlling, blaming and critical.

This book is not intended to offer a deep examination of transactional analysis or psychotherapy which is where this model originated. Quite apart from anything else, I am completely unqualified to do so. But used sensitively, the drama triangle can be a useful way for you to help your coachee gain some perspective on the different roles they or other individuals may be playing.

I can remember a coaching conversation with someone I thought was playing – albeit unwittingly – the role of rescuer in a situation at work. They weren't really helping the other person, let's call him Mark, who was in difficulty, because all my coachee was doing was offering sympathy and a shoulder to cry on. What she wasn't doing was helping Mark to own his situation and stand up to the person bullying him. By asking questions like: 'What are the pros and cons of the approach you are taking with Mark?' I allowed her to see for herself how her approach could change for the better. We could then focus on working out how she could do this.

The next chapter focuses on a key element that links to the difference between empathy and sympathy: your ability to stay positive.

BASIC QUESTIONS

✓ I'd be interested to understand this better. What are you thinking?
✓ How do you think this happened?
✓ How has that left you feeling?
✓ I sense this is difficult. What would help the situation?
✓ I'm wondering what you think you can do about this?
✓ I am starting to get a sense of what's important here for you. What's at the heart of the issue?
✓ This sounds tough. When you have dug deep before, what helped you?
✓ Let's explore what you can do. Who is in a position to help with this?
✓ You seem rather deflated by this?
✓ I'd like to understand more about this. What do you think could unlock the situation for you?

BASIC REVIEW

✓ How is emotional intelligence important in helping you build a strong relationship with your coachee?
✓ What role does empathy play within emotional intelligence?
✓ How empathetic do you think you are?
✓ How do you know?
✓ What is the difference between empathy and sympathy?
✓ How good are you at avoiding sympathy when necessary?
✓ What is the drama triangle?
✓ How well do you empower others rather than rescue them?
✓ What has been most useful about this chapter for you?

NOTES

9

Stay Positive

When I am coaching I usually have two goals in mind whether it's at work or in a home situation: I want my coachee to feel even *clearer* and more *optimistic* (than they already are) about the future.

When it comes to creating greater clarity, the BASIC steps method provides a powerful pathway to help your coachee reflect on their situation, identify what they want to achieve, sort through their options, and decide what to do. Of course, this in itself will leave them feeling more optimistic, but experience has taught me that a sense of optimism doesn't just come from having clarity about the future; it is rooted in the way in which the conversation itself has taken place.

In the last 20 years or so our knowledge and understanding of the importance of taking a more positive approach to personal development, growth and well-being has increased enormously.

POSITIVE PSYCHOLOGY

✓ We should pay more attention to the positives in life than the problems.
✓ About building the positive emotions of hope, kindness and gratitude.

APPRECIATIVE ENQUIRY

✓ All about seeking out the positives in situations rather than the problems that need to be solved.
✓ Focus on imagining a positive future.

SOLUTIONS-FOCUSED

✓ Focus on 'what works' in a situation.
✓ Not dependent on knowing the cause of a problem.
✓ If something doesn't work, try something different.

PLAYING TO STRENGTHS

✓ Focusing on what individuals are good at rather than their weaknesses.
✓ Leveraging these specific strengths, alongside the strengths of others, to plan for a positive future.

There are various different schools of thinking is this area, but they all share some common under-pinning principles:

- We should focus on the possibilities not on the problem.
- There is a powerful link between the language we hear and use and our own emotions.
- The power of positive thought to change our emotional state should not be underestimated.

As a former boss of mine Jon Coles used to say: 'There are times, Andy, when as leaders we just need to show *unwarranted optimism*. There is no reason to be optimistic just now. But there will be.' Jon is the CEO of United Learning, currently the largest academy group in the country, and I worked with him as the managing director of schools. It's not that we shouldn't acknowledge when things are difficult, far from it, but we need to keep the faith that we can do something about what needs fixing. I can think of many coaching conversations where just framing questions positively has changed the whole dynamic of the discussion. A senior executive in a financial services company was grappling with a major project to change the key operating system the whole company used. Like many IT projects, the context was complex, at risk of unforeseen costs and with some colleagues being resistant to change. I asked her some questions like:

- When was the last time you faced an issue like this and overcame it?
- What have you achieved so far?
- Who are the people that will be part of successfully completing this project?
- How can you play to each person's strengths?

These helped her refocus on the positives of her situation and think about the future with more optimism and self-belief.

Using time effectively

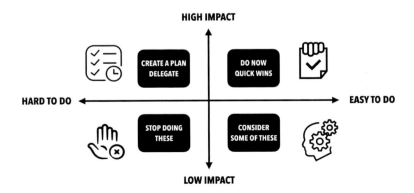

I was recently in a conversation with a headteacher who was feeling quite overwhelmed by the sheer volume of work he was having to cope with. While it was important to allow him some space to just let off some steam, when it felt like the time was right I started with some questions that helped him focus on the positives of the situation. Asking: 'When you are good at prioritising your time, what do you do?' enabled him to feel like he could regain some control. Then using the simple prioritisation model above to help him structure his thinking, he was able to practically map out how he was going to manage the workload and feel more on top of things.

Using EARS

In *The solutions focus* Jackson and McKergrow introduce us to the acronym EARS as another great way to think about how we prompt more positive thinking through how we ask and listen.

ELICIT
AMPLIFY
REINFORCE
START

Elicit

This is an opportunity to get your coachee to focus on and explain the positives of their situation or what they may have done before that has worked in similar situations.

Amplify

This involves getting them to play back what they have said, with a particular focus or emphasis on the things that might be useful to bear in mind with their new challenge or goal. It can help to ask questions like: 'Tell me a bit more about what you did that worked. Why did it work so well, do you think?' Note that the *why* question here is fine because it is unambiguously *positive*.

Reinforce

This is where you reinforce the positives of the situation. You might say: 'That sounds like it was really successful. It can't have been easy, but you pulled it off – well done.' It's a chance to keep building positivity.

Start (over)

The process of building a positive narrative never finishes. Take the opportunity to explore more of the positives from a situation and the strengths exhibited by the individuals concerned. It's the equivalent of asking 'and what else?' about the positives of a situation.

Review and celebrate the positives

In *The leader's guide to coaching in schools*, John Campbell and Christian van Nieuwerburgh remind us of the importance of the celebration of success. Sometimes this may relate to gains that may have been achieved within the conversation itself. On other occasions, it may be a positive look forward to the successes on the horizon. In either case, the focus is on the positive things that have or will be achieved. In his book *The happiness advantage*, Shawn Achor says that because *positive brains* have a biological advantage over brains that are neutral or negative, this teaches us the importance of retraining our brains to capitalise on positivity and improve our productivity and performance.

Keep it real

I have seen some coaches take the idea of keeping positive one step too far. This usually involves inauthentic praise or unwarranted positive praise. There is a big difference between keeping positive and optimistic, and offering what Kim Scott would, as we saw in Chapter 5 (BASIC Implementation), call ruinous empathy. This is where you are so fixed on keeping positive and not upsetting someone that you fail to say what they need to hear. This is, of course, where the judgment of a coach comes into play.

The next chapter is the first in the BASIC Habits section of the book and relates to a fundamental habit in the BASIC model: ask first.

BASIC QUESTIONS

- ✓ What are you most proud of that you have achieved since we last spoke?
- ✓ What have you tried so far that seems to be working?
- ✓ Who can help you with this?
- ✓ What are your natural strengths that it might be useful to take advantage of in this situation?
- ✓ Tell me what this would look like if you achieved it?
- ✓ How would it make you feel if you achieved this?
- ✓ OK, great that you have a choice here; what are you thinking might work best?
- ✓ What do you think would be the right thing to do first?
- ✓ Out of ten, how clear are you about what you need to do to make this happen?
- ✓ How do you think your team would feel if this worked well?
- ✓ What's been the most useful thing about this conversation for you?

BASIC REVIEW

- ✓ How do you ensure that your coachee leaves conversations with you feeling clearer and more optimistic about the future?
- ✓ Do you try to focus on the possibilities and not the problems?
- ✓ Have you experienced how the whole dynamic of a conversation can change if you adopt a positive approach to your coaching?
- ✓ How might you use the prioritisation model in your coaching?
- ✓ How could the EARS model help you build more positivity into your conversations?
- ✓ How do you make sure you don't drift into *ruinous empathy* by offering inauthentic praise or unwarranted positive feedback?
- ✓ What has been most useful about this chapter for you?

NOTES

10

Ask First

In case you were wondering, this is not a chapter about asking for permission! It's the first of four chapters looking at key coaching habits. This first chapter is really about how you can develop a coaching habit in your everyday interactions with people, rather than just in more formal coaching conversations.

When colleagues or family members come to you for help or advice, you probably only have *three types* of conversation.

Type 1: You end up with a job

In the first type of conversation, before you know it, you've ended up with a job! Of course, there is a time and place when this is appropriate; if something is high risk and looking like it is about to go wrong, you may well need to step in. If someone is really stressed for some reason and can't cope, you might just need to help. But if your habit is to take on jobs from others without thinking, you are probably taking on more than you should. I remember when I was head of year in school I used to let a huge number of monkeys jump on my back. On reflection there were various reasons this tended to happen: because I genuinely wanted to help out someone who I could see was very busy or struggling with something; because I wanted the other person to think I was capable and good at my job; and finally because I often found myself thinking it would just be quicker and easier to do something myself. But as the direction of the arrow on the model implies, while there is a place for type one conversations, you shouldn't have too many.

Type 2: You offer advice

I would suggest you can afford to have a few more of the second type of conversation. These are dialogues in which you end up giving advice, making suggestions or even just telling someone what to do. At least with these, you don't end up taking something on, and hopefully the other person will be able to apply what they have learned from the conversation in the future. But if they keep coming back to you with similar questions, and if you continue to just answer them, they can become over-dependent upon you when it comes to making decisions. In this situation, these conversations don't build capacity or competence in other people at work or at home. In fact, they do the reverse.

Type 3: You ask questions

In the third type of conversation, you just ask great questions. Initially, these help you understand the situation; both the context and an individual's capacity to manage it. Only then do you decide how best to proceed. If at this point you need to intervene and take the job off them or give them advice, then that's fine. You have made a conscious decision to do that, not out of habit, but because it's what the situation requires. There is also the added benefit that the quality of your advice will be better because you know more about the situation. If you both have the time, spending a tiny bit longer on the conversation and staying in questioning mode can very often help people work out for themselves what they need to do. These mini-coaching conversations don't have to take long; it's more about you using a coaching leadership style than it is actual formal coaching. You will be surprised, even in a five-minute conversation, how much ground can be covered. You leave the conversation with no task to undertake. The other person leaves feeling they have been properly listened to and having had the opportunity to think through the situation. They are also less likely to ask you the same question again next time.

Asking first

If you start all your conversations by asking great questions, you are giving colleagues the chance to work out their own solutions. If you subsequently realise that they aren't able to work out what to do (or if time is short) you may decide you need to intervene further, and that's absolutely fine. You are consciously using the approach that suits the situation, rather than just diving in with advice or taking the job from them. In other words, by asking first in all your conversations, without even thinking about it, you have a much greater chance of adopting the right approach in every conversation you have.

Link with the coaching continuum

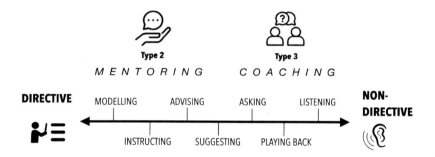

As you may remember, the coaching continuum sets out the range of different types of conversation we have with one another. If you think about it, having type three conversations is really the equivalent of coaching, whereas in type two conversations, you are effectively mentoring.

Link with leadership styles

In *Leadership that gets results*, Daniel Goleman recaps for us the concept of leadership styles that he first published in his research into the topic back in 2000. It's not the only model of this kind but for me it has stood the test of time.

I am sharing it here for two reasons: (i) because there are real parallels with the coaching continuum and the range of approaches you can use in coaching, and (ii) because Goleman's model is a powerful model for any leader you may be coaching to use to think about how to adapt their leadership approach to suit the context they are working in.

Goleman identifies six key leadership styles, and these are summarised below.

Visionary

Primary objective: providing long term direction and vision. You tend to:

♦ develop and articulate a clear vision
♦ solicit staff perspectives on the vision and see selling the vision as key to success
♦ persuade staff by explaining the rationale for the team's best long-term interests
♦ set standards and monitor performance in relation to the wider vision
♦ motivate with a balance of positive and negative feedback.

Affiliative

Primary objective: creating staff harmony. You tend to:

♦ be concerned with promoting friendly interactions
♦ place more emphasis on addressing staff needs than on goals and standards
♦ pay attention to, and care for, the whole person; stress things that keep people happy
♦ avoid performance related confrontations
♦ reward personal characteristics more than job performance.

Directive

Primary objective: compliance. You tend to:

- give lots of directives, not direction
- expect immediate staff compliance
- control tightly
- rely on negative, corrective feedback
- motivate by imposing sanctions for non-compliance, with few rewards
- rarely explain rationale, only negative consequences.

Democratic

Primary objective: building commitment and generating new ideas. You tend to:

- trust that staff can develop the appropriate direction for themselves and the organisation
- invite staff to participate in decisions
- reach decisions by consensus
- delegate decision-making as well as tasks
- hold many meetings and listen to staff concerns
- reward adequate performance; rarely give negative feedback.

Pacesetting

Primary objective: making rapid progress with excellence. You tend to:

- lead by example and have high standards: 'look at me; do what I am doing; keep up with me'
- expect others to know the rationale behind what is being modelled
- be apprehensive about delegating
- take responsibility away if high performance is not forthcoming, and have little sympathy for poor performance
- rescue the situation or give detailed task instructions when staff experience difficulties.

Coaching

Primary objective: long term professional development of others. You tend to:

- help staff identify their unique strengths and weaknesses
- encourage staff to establish long range development goals
- reach agreement with staff on the team leader's and individuals' roles in the development process
- provide on-going advice and feedback
- sometimes trade off immediate standards of performance for long-term development.

Sometimes an individual, team or organisation can need a very directional approach from a leader, particularly if it isn't functioning well. If your coachee is working with individuals who are not operating as a unit and where performance is variable, they may just need to say: 'We need to do it like this'. This approach is all about taking charge and setting out in detail what needs to happen.

In contrast, a high performing team would find such an approach completely de-motivating; coming in and just telling people what to do would be very likely to leave them feeling frustrated and under-valued.

Knowing which style is best used with the team as a whole, or with individuals within it, is where you can help your coachee exercise the professional judgement and emotional awareness needed to get their leadership style right.

What is important is that you give them the time and space to consciously think about which approach they want to use. You may find the diagram overleaf a useful prompt in such conversations.

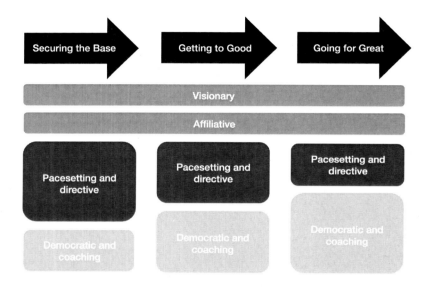

When it comes to thinking about the typical journey of improvement most individuals, teams and organisations go through, I have come up with the three stages of (i) securing the base, (ii) getting to good and (iii) going for great. In all three stages a visionary and affiliative leadership style will probably be very useful. Why wouldn't your coachee want to focus on the future with their team and on building strong relationships within it? These styles are useful in any context. The balance between the other four styles probably needs to change as experience grows and performance improves.

While a coachee may need to be quite pacesetting and directive at the start of an improvement journey, this requirement ought to decline over time. Simultaneously, your coachee will probably want to gradually increase how much they use the democratic and coaching leadership styles, as they build capacity and trust in their team.

I can remember one conversation I had with a coachee who seemed to be stuck in directive mode. It seemed as if she had failed to notice that the context she was working in had evolved and things had really started to improve. By going into mentor mode and sharing this model with her, I was able to return to coaching and support her to see for herself that she needed to become less directive in her leadership approach. Too often, leaders can get stuck with the leadership habits that have served them well at the start of their journey and fail to make this kind of adjustment along the way.

The best way to avoid this is of course to get leaders doing exactly what we recommend all coaches do: ask first!

The next chapter will examine how tiny differences in the way you ask or frame your questions can make a huge difference to the effectiveness of your coaching.

BASIC QUESTIONS

- ✓ What's on your mind?
- ✓ What is the performance currently like?
- ✓ Tell me about the people involved?
- ✓ If you were going to rate each out of ten, what would you give them?
- ✓ What do you want to achieve?
- ✓ At a high level, what's the right approach to take here?
- ✓ What's going to be the right leadership style for this situation?
- ✓ What do you need to do to make this happen?
- ✓ If you are saying yes to this, what are you saying no to?
- ✓ What are the chances you are actually going to be successful at this?
- ✓ What could stop this working?

BASIC REVIEW

- ✓ What were the three types of conversation in the *ask first* model?
- ✓ What will be the benefit for your coachees if you always *ask first*?
- ✓ How can you develop the habit of *asking first*?
- ✓ How do you think both the *ask first* model and Daniel Goleman's *leadership styles* model link with the coaching continuum?
- ✓ How might you use Daniel Goleman's *leadership styles* model as part of your own coaching approach when you are talking with leaders?
- ✓ What has been most useful about this chapter for you?

NOTES

11

Frame Well

The more I reflect on my own coaching and the more I read about the subject, the more I have come to realise that it can often be the smallest of differences in the way we frame our questions that can transform the impact of our coaching. This chapter aims to share with you a series of key lessons I have learned; the common mistakes that I and many other coaches have made on our coaching journeys. To bring these lessons to life, in some of the areas I have included 'before and after' scenarios to really try to exemplify what things looks like in practice when we

frame well. As you are working your way through these suggestions, you may find it useful to be thinking about each one in terms of your own coaching and the extent to which you may need to focus on a particular example. We all bring our own pre-dispositions to coaching. Some of the pitfalls I am suggesting you avoid will apply to you more than others.

Keep right

The fundamental piece of advice I would like to offer is to stay on the right-hand-side of the coaching continuum for *as long as you can* and trust the coaching process. In my early coaching I was too ready to move to the left, often without even knowing I was doing it. As you will see from some of the examples I am sharing in this chapter, we may technically be asking questions, but in reality we are actually in mentor mode.

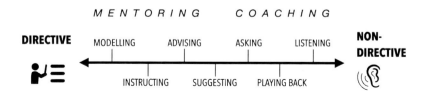

How you do this will ultimately be up to you to work out for yourself, but the rest of this chapter contains a series of practical strategies you may wish to consider.

Keep your questions open

You will no doubt be familiar with the difference between the open and the closed question. Open questions allow your coachee lots of freedom and space to think and explore possibilities. Closed questions limit their thinking or try to point them in a particular direction or towards a particular action. As you look at the examples given below there are a couple of things to note:

- Questions that start with *what* or *how* are generally likely to be open.
- Questions where *you* is the second word are very often closed.

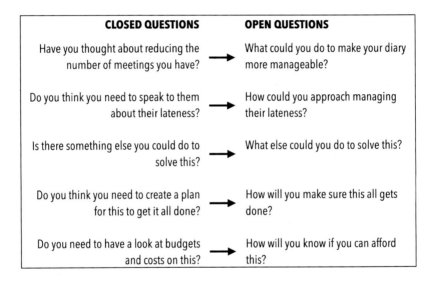

CLOSED QUESTIONS	OPEN QUESTIONS
Have you thought about reducing the number of meetings you have?	What could you do to make your diary more manageable?
Do you think you need to speak to them about their lateness?	How could you approach managing their lateness?
Is there something else you could do to solve this?	What else could you do to solve this?
Do you think you need to create a plan for this to get it all done?	How will you make sure this all gets done?
Do you need to have a look at budgets and costs on this?	How will you know if you can afford this?

The closed questions above are all, whether intentionally or not, leading your coachee in a particular direction. The open questions on the right give them ownership and freedom to come up with their own ideas.

Try variations on an AWEsome theme

We have already discussed the power of: '**A**nd **w**hat **e**lse?' to really push your coachee to think beyond the obvious. But it can start to sound a little unnatural if you keep repeating the phrase.

Here are some alternatives that work equally well:

- ◆ Tell me more?
- ◆ Can you expand on that?
- ◆ What's another option here?
- ◆ How else could you do this?
- ◆ What other ideas do you have?

Use *what* not *why*

As we have already explored, asking *why* can often result in a defensive response from your coachee. Even though you may be genuinely interested in why they have chosen to do something in a particular way, it can often feel like you are judging them if the question starts with *why*. Usually, reframing questions to start with *what* can do the trick. Here are a few examples to illustrate what I mean.

WHY	WHAT
Why did you do this? →	What were the circumstances that led you to do this?
Why don't you just talk to them about this? →	What has stopped you talking to them up to now?
Why are you anxious about this? →	What is it that is making you anxious about this?
Why have you chosen this option? →	What makes this option your preferred choice?
Why aren't you getting on with this person? →	What lies behind your difficult relationship with this person?

All the questions on the left have the potential for your coachee to feel as if you have some form of negative perception of what they think or have done. The *what* questions on the right are not a cast-iron guarantee this won't happen, but they go a long way to suggesting you are interested and curious.

Talk less, listen more

As a rule of thumb, if you are talking for more than 20% of the time you have probably moved from coach to mentor mode. As we said before, if that is your deliberate intention and your coachee has agreed to you sharing some ideas, models or possible solutions, then that is absolutely fine. But if you want to be in coaching mode and you are doing all the talking, something is clearly wrong. Remember, coaching is about your coachee doing the work, not you. If you have a tendency to talk too much you may not even know you do it. Thinking about how you can get a sense of this might be worth exploring. Some coaches agree with their coachees to record conversations occasionally so they can hear or watch themselves back and reflect on what has happened.

Go with the flow

Don't be too rigid with the structure of the conversation. Religiously following the BASIC Steps structure, for example, can make a conversation feel quite artificial and stilted for your coachee. As we have already discussed, it is often a good idea to revisit certain parts of a conversation. Here are some examples of when this can be useful:

- When your coachee is wandering off track, asking them about the aim can help them refocus.
- When you are discussing what actions they want to take as part of the implementation phase, and they seem to be creating a new overall strategy.

Going back and reconfirming the strategy can bring useful clarity to their approach.

◆ When your coachee is struggling to come up with what they want to do, going back to the background and some of the positives they can build from can help prompt them to come up with new ideas.

◆ When they don't seem that committed to carrying out what they have decided to do, getting them to reflect back on the aim and how they will feel when it's achieved can be a powerful motivator.

Remember it's their outcome

This may seem an odd thing to say, but I can think of many occasions when I have become so wrapped up in a coaching conversation that I forgot that it was not my issue but my coachee's that we were discussing! Apart from the fact that this can lead you to inadvertently ask more closed questions, it also means you lose that ability to be the slightly detached observer in the situation.

This, after all, is one of the key benefits of coaching: having someone who is not part of the context challenging you to reflect and decide for the best, less encumbered by personal history, emotions and potential bias.

Get the tone right

Try to keep the tone of your questions in line with the overall feel and flow of the conversation. If you are too formal for example, your coachee may find it harder to relax or open up. Conversely, if you are too casual your coachee may feel that you aren't taking them seriously. This point links to the *match-pace-lead* model we will discuss in the next chapter.

Ask one question at a time

This may sound like a really obvious point, but it never ceases to amaze me how often I catch myself asking more than one question at a time. Sometimes this is when I'm trying to re-frame the original question because I'm not happy with it. On other occasions it is because I'm jumping ahead with the line of enquiry, almost pre-judging what a coachee may be going to say. What seems to help me avoid this trap is to just slow down and remember there is no rush. Just take your time, trust the process and ask one question at a time.

Silence is golden

Silence is OK. In fact, resisting the temptation to fill what may feel like an awkward moment can create the space for when the very best thinking often happens. This is particularly hard if you have already thought about what you want to say next. This in itself though can be a useful indicator of how well you are suspending your own view of the world and entering your coachee's. If you do find yourself thinking of your next question in the middle of your coachee's answer, you probably aren't really engaging in the deeper listening we explore in the next chapter on *listening well.*

BASIC QUESTIONS

- ✓ What could you do to make this more manageable?
- ✓ How could you approach managing this?
- ✓ What else could you do to solve this?
- ✓ How will you make sure this all gets done?
- ✓ How will you know if you can afford this?
- ✓ What were the circumstances that lead you to do this?
- ✓ What has stopped you doing this up to now?
- ✓ What is it that is making you anxious about this?
- ✓ What makes this option your preferred choice?
- ✓ What lies behind your difficult relationship with this person?

BASIC REVIEW

- ✓ How well do you manage the temptation to go into advice-giving mode?
- ✓ How useful do you think asking open questions rather than closed questions could be for you?
- ✓ How can asking *what* not *why* help your coaching?
- ✓ What are the benefits of talking less and listening more?
- ✓ How well do you remember the outcomes are your coachee's not yours?
- ✓ How can you ensure the tone of what you say is appropriate?
- ✓ How well do you ask one question at a time?
- ✓ What are the benefits of silence in coaching conversations?

NOTES

12

Listen Hard

BASIC STEPS   BASIC QUALITIES   **BASIC HABITS**   BASIC FEEDBACK

ASK FIRST   FRAME WELL   **LISTEN HARD**   PLAY BACK

Reading this book up to now, you could be forgiven for thinking that great coaching is all about asking great questions in the right order and in the right way. All of that is of course true, but it's not the full story. Even if your questioning is superb, if you don't listen well, you will be missing the opportunity to be even more effective. Great listening is about properly suspending your own view of the world and really trying to understand your coachee's perspective. As Henry Ford said: 'If there is any great secret of success in life, it lies in the ability to put yourself in another person's place and to see things from their point of view.'

Listening is active not passive

The first thing about listening is that it is active not passive. When done well, listening gives you information about a situation or individual, and leads you towards greater insight, awareness and learning. You might see a different perspective or clarify your thinking. Of course, active listening relies on good questioning. By structuring your questions in the way I have suggested, you can lead someone through a thinking process or suggest new ways of approaching a problem. How well do you tend to structure your questions at the moment? How do they provide enough space for the other person to reflect?

You can also listen and pick up information that goes beyond the words being used. You can 'listen' for emotion, body language, tone of voice, speed of talking and clarity of thinking. By listening actively for these, you can discern a great deal about the other person's frame of mind, emotional state, and the purpose of the conversation. Often the words someone is using do not reflect what they really mean or want to say. How far do you listen beyond the words for what is really behind a conversation, what isn't being said?

In her book *More time to think*, Nancy Kline talks about creating a 'thinking environment' for a person by listening to them in what she calls a generative way, with a totally positive disposition towards the individual. It starts with a 'What do you think?' type question. You are curious and interested. When the person runs out of steam, she suggests you need to ask: 'And what else are you thinking?' You can see the similarity here with the work of Bungay-Stanier and his AWEsome

'And what else?' question. Giving someone space and time to think is liberating for them and can lead to them solving their own issues in an environment set by the coach. Nancy's book is well worth a read.

How to show you are listening

Others are more likely to open up and share what they really think if they feel you are properly listening to them. To a certain extent, simply how relevant you make your questions will demonstrate that you are listening, but there are other techniques you can use:

- Reflecting back the words someone has used or making statements showing you understand their emotions.
- Your body language and tone of voice can mirror the non-verbal signals someone is giving, so if they are angry you might choose to change your body language and tone of voice to be less confrontational.
- If they are upset you might again change your demeanour to elicit a different response.

For example, if someone seems quite deflated in what they are saying, in their tone or body-language, you can show you are listening by adjusting your own approach to fit.

Match – pace – lead

This simple technique has its roots in neuro-linguistic programming (NLP) although I happen to think it is just a bit of common sense. The basic idea is that at the beginning of a conversation you need to *match* your coachee: in your overall level of energy; in your choice of vocabulary; in your body-language. You will agree on things with them and be very affirming. You will probably find that if you start matching some of your coachee's language back to them, particularly relating to their beliefs and values, your rapport with them will grow. You can say things such as, 'So you believe that...?' 'You said that...' 'We are agreed, then, that...?'

Match ••••••▶ **Pace** ••••••▶ **Lead**

The idea is that you continue with this for a while – keeping the same *pace* – which settles the conversation into a natural flow between the two of you.

When you feel the time is right, you shift the energy level, content or tone to where you think it needs to be to help lift your coachee towards their goal. This more advanced coaching technique isn't one I would recommend coaches focus on at the start of their coaching journey, although all of us do it to some extent without even realising it.

Having an awareness of the differences in communication and processing styles between you and the person you are communicating with is essential. To be an effective listener, it's important to be calm and create enough space to listen and absorb what is being said. If you are too busy talking and preparing what you will say next, how will you know what is really being said to you? This skill of being able to think and listen at the same time is an important one to develop to be an effective coach.

So, as well as asking great questions in the right order and in the right way, you need to listen well. How, then, do you know if you are listening well? One way can be to think about your level of listening.

Levels of listening

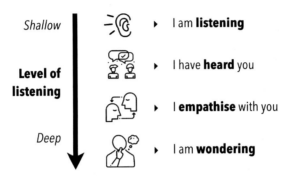

Shallow — ▶ I am **listening**

Level of listening — ▶ I have **heard** you

▶ I **empathise** with you

Deep — ▶ I am **wondering**

I am listening
At its most basic, you can show someone you are listening by showing attentiveness though nodding and occasional verbal cues.

I have heard
To let your coachee know that not only have you listened but you have *heard*, it can be very powerful to play back what you have heard. More on this in the next chapter. In its simplest form, this is a statement that starts with something along the lines of: 'It sounds like what you are saying is….'.

I empathise with you
The next level of listening involves you saying something which shows not only that you have heard, but that you can *empathise* with their situation. This can

sometimes be communicated through your body language or tone of voice, or it may be through what you say. Your response might begin with: 'This really reminds me of when...'. This is an opportunity to say something from your own experience that shows you have some idea of what it must be like to be in their position.

Two big health warnings come with this approach, however: (i) remember the conversation is about them; don't go on too long about your own story – it needs to be just long enough for them to appreciate that you can empathise with their situation; (ii) always make sure you preface your remarks with the recognition that your situation isn't exactly the same as theirs.

I am wondering
The deepest level of listening, sometimes referred to as generative empathetic listening, is when you make a statement that includes something that you haven't actually heard them say; something that your intuition is telling you on the basis of what you have heard. I often start a statement like this with: 'I'm just wondering if...'. I can remember one of the conversations with my Uncle Peter where he was telling me all the reasons why he didn't want to have a hot meal delivered each lunchtime to his home.

My intuition was telling me there was more to it than that. I just said to him 'I'm just wondering if all this talk of home lunch deliveries is making you worried that we think you can't manage on your own and may need to go into a home'. He said it was. My response was to ask whether he thought having home meals might be a way he could stay in his own home for longer. He paused for a moment (I have learned that like most of us, he needs time and space to think, something I hadn't always given him). 'Yes, Andy. I suppose you are right'. We then went to explore the various options open to him.

BASIC REVIEW

✓ Why is *listening well* a really important element of the BASIC coaching method?
✓ How can you ensure that listening is a proactive not a passive activity in your coaching?
✓ How can you show you are listening?
✓ How can you use match-pace-lead to build rapport and inject energy, when appropriate?
✓ Looking at the four levels of listening model, where you you think you tend to operate the most?
✓ How might this model help you to improve your listening during coaching?
✓ What has been most useful about this chapter for you?

NOTES

NOTES

13

Play Back

One of the elements of my own coaching that I really underestimated in the early days was the power of playing back what a coachee has said. A powerful component of an effective coaching conversation at work or at home is repeating back what you have heard, often summarising the main points your coachee has made. Organising your coachee's thoughts for them and sharing them back in this way can greatly improve the coaching process.

So in simple terms this is a three-stage process within a coaching conversation. You begin by asking some questions that get your coachee thinking. Throughout this, you listen well in the way we described in the previous chapter. Finally, you play back what you have heard. By doing this, there are three key benefits that usually emerge, emphasising why this is such a powerful technique to use.

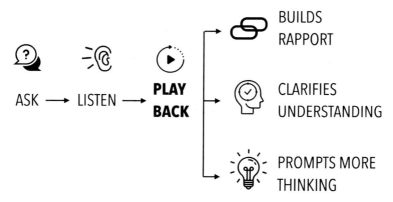

Builds rapport

Firstly, taking the time and trouble to play back what you have heard sends a very clear message to your coachee that not only have you been listening, but that you have heard what they have said. You are immediately at the second level of listening. When I am talking with my Uncle Peter, I can tell he loves it when I do this just from the tone of his voice, especially because I suspect that he sometimes thinks I don't listen to him or take on board his views. This is a great way to build rapport.

Clarifies understanding

Not only does playing back what you have heard build rapport, it is a useful way to check that you have understood the main points your coachee is making. This can be particularly important towards the end of the *background* step in a conversation. It gives your coachee a chance to correct any misconceptions you might have had, or review a part of the dialogue you have missed, which they think is significant. Another point where playing back can be very useful is towards the end of the *strategy* step in a conversation. Hopefully your coachee, with your prompting, will have come up with a number of possible approaches to take. Playing those back to them can provide a succinct summary from which they can decide the strategy to pursue.

Prompts a further thought

The final major advantage of playing back is that it nearly always results in another thought or response from your coachee. When you try this yourself, I can pretty much guarantee that the response you will get from your coachee with start with: 'Yes, and…' or 'Yes, but…'. In other words, your coachee will agree with your summary but either qualify it in some way or use your synthesis to have a brand-new thought or idea. I love it when this happens in a coaching conversation, it's at the heart of why having a conversation with someone else rather than just thinking on your own is such a powerful way to gain clarity and build optimism.

Offers a stepping stone

As we have already seen with the examples above, a useful time to play back what you have heard is often towards the end of one of the BASIC steps in a conversation. It offers a natural bridge between ending one phase of the conversation and starting another. When I think about a conversation I had recently with my Uncle Peter, we were talking about what his options were for getting a hot lunch now that he wasn't able to get to the pub. I summarised for him the three options we had been discussing. Not only did he find the reminder useful, it immediately got him thinking about his preference. In other words, we were tying up the final stage of *strategy* and were now ready to move into *implementation*.

BASIC QUESTIONS

- ✓ It sounds like…
- ✓ I'm wondering if what you mean is…
- ✓ Have I understood this correctly? Are you saying…
- ✓ If I have heard this right, you seem to be saying…
- ✓ You seem to be suggesting… Tell me more about that.
- ✓ If I summarise what you have just said, I am wondering if…
- ✓ You have said the following three key things… Which of those is the most important?
- ✓ Do you mean…?
- ✓ If it's true that… what does this mean for what you might want to do?
- ✓ Your key strategies seem to be… Which do you think will work best in this situation?
- ✓ You have said you need to… Which one will you do first?

 # BASIC REVIEW

- ✓ How could developing the habit of playing back be a powerful addition to your coaching repertoire?
- ✓ How does playing back build rapport between you and your coachee?
- ✓ If playing back is a great way to check that you have understood and allows your coachee the chance to correct any misconceptions or omissions, how could you ensure you do this more often?
- ✓ Have you had an experience where playing back has prompted a further thought or idea?
- ✓ From your experience, how can playing back provide a natural bridge between one BASIC step to the next?
- ✓ What has been most useful about this chapter for you?

NOTES

14

Make Connections

The final section of this book will focus on giving feedback. You may be wondering why I have included this topic in a book on coaching. In fact, when I was first introduced to the idea of feedback as something that was somehow part of using a coaching approach, I was pretty sceptical. Now, however, I am absolutely convinced of its place within a wider view of what constitutes coaching.

If we take another look at the coaching continuum, we can see how some of the elements towards the left-hand side are relevant when it comes to feedback. After all, giving feedback is all about offering suggestions or giving advice about how something could improve.

As we discussed in the introduction, while a coaching approach to conversations can be a very powerful tool, there are clearly times when giving some advice is the right thing to do.

If you find yourself in a situation as a coach where you are starting to feel that no matter how many questions you ask, your coachee isn't going to be able to work out what to do, of course you are going to offer some advice or show them how to do something. Why would you deliberately withhold advice when your greater knowledge and experience means you have the answer they need?

In his book *Leverage Leadership*, Paul Bambrick-Santoyo identifies five key areas (summarised opposite) where what we often think about feedback may not be right. Although he is writing here about how teachers give feedback to one another on their teaching, I think his ideas are applicable in most feedback situations.

- Lots of feedback is good
- Detailed reports are important
- Just tell them and they'll get it
- State the action and they'll know what to do
- They can do what needs to be done at any time

What we often **think**

- Less feedback is much better
- Most of us prefer a short face-to-face chat
- Better to get them to do the thinking
- Show them how to do stuff
- Nail down the timings

What is actually **true**

So, what are the key ideas from Bambrick-Santoyo's work when it comes to what you can do to help your coachee improve?

- ◆ Help your coachee prioritise what they are going to focus on; trying to improve in too many areas at once isn't really that helpful as we end up not getting better at any of them.
- ◆ While there is a place for a written summary of feedback – as this can allow someone to revisit it – when it comes to leveraging change, most of us would find sitting down and having a positive and future-focused conversation more useful.
- ◆ It is always better to start trying to identify potential areas for growth by asking your coachee to reflect for themselves first; only if they cannot see what you have seen should you tell them.
- ◆ When it comes to working out what to do differently, don't be afraid to move into mentor mode if they need you to.
- ◆ Make sure you have agreed some clear timeframes about what will be achieved and by when.

These ideas will inform what I will be sharing in this chapter and the next.

The feedback sandwich

Much has been written about how to give great feedback. You have probably heard of the feedback sandwich. You may even have another name for it! I am increasingly of the view that the traditional feedback sandwich may have had its day.

The idea behind the feedback sandwich is a good one. Make sure there is some positive stuff in among your feedback. In fact, make sure there is more positive than negative, and ensure there is something to improve or develop. All of which is great. The trouble with this approach is that individuals don't really own their area for growth, even though they may well have ideas about how they can improve which might be pretty similar. Or they may not agree with what the person offering feedback thinks. My response has instead been to apply the *ask first* mantra outlined in Chapter 10 to feedback, which has resulted in me coming up with a new approach called *Mind your Ps and Qs.*

Mind your Ps and Qs

We all know what this rather old-fashioned phrase means, it's about being polite; about minding our 'pleases' and 'thank qs'. No one is completely certain of the origin of the phrase, but it has certainly been around for a while. Apparently in the seventeenth century, pub landlords would be expected to make sure that their patrons *minded their pints and quarts* and didn't get too drunk! Whatever its origin, I have taken the phrase and used it as a great way to make a connection with someone when you are giving feedback that has all the benefits of the feedback sandwich but without its disadvantages. One of the biggest challenges with giving developmental or critical feedback is that people can often get very defensive. This is why, in the minding your Ps and Qs model, that the P stands for *positive*.

In other words, you start your feedback conversation with some really positive things you have seen, heard or noticed. Like any good praise, it needs to be specific, authentic and meaningful. There is nothing worse than the ubiquitous 'That was great!' You are left thinking *what* was great? Why was it great? Did you even really mean that?

 POSITIVE
✓ Specific
P ✓ Authentic

 QUESTION
✓ Curious
Q ✓ Challenging

Once you have shared the positives, you can ask them for their positives; what they are pleased about. There may well be something that that you haven't noticed or realised.

The next step is to move onto the areas for growth or development. In this stage, the Q is all about asking *curious* questions such as: 'What did you notice about...?' or 'What do you think was happening at this point...?' or making statements such as 'I was wondering if...'. In other words, you are getting them to reflect for themselves on what the areas for development might be. This has several advantages:

- ◆ They are more likely to own the areas for growth.
- ◆ They are less likely to be defensive about what can improve.
- ◆ They are more likely to be committed to making a positive change in the area that has been identified.

Move from open to closed questions

As with most coaching conversations, it is usually most useful if you start by asking more open questions that allow your coachee to explore possibilities for themselves. However, when you want them to focus on the specifics of what they want to do, or if they are having difficulty in seeing what you think might be a powerful place to focus their attention, you may want to ask more of a closed or leading question. This is where your questions can really challenge your coachee to think hard about something, but with them being much less likely to feel threatened or defensive. For example, good open questions early on could be: 'What could you do differently next time?' or 'What didn't work out quite how you hoped?' More closed questions might start with: 'Are you happy with what you have come up with?' or 'When are you going to do this?'

If all else fails – just tell them!

No matter how skilled you are at asking great questions, we all know there are times when you can keep asking questions until you have exhausted all possible lines of enquiry and still someone hasn't seen what needs to change. In this situation, of course you need to tell someone what your own views are, but at least you have given them the chance to work things out for themselves first.

As I mentioned earlier, this is just another example where you are asking first and only offering advice as a conscious decision. You can recap this idea in Chapter 10 (Ask First). It also draws on Kim Scott's principle of *radical candour* discussed in Chapter 5 (BASIC Commitment) which emphasises the importance of the person knowing you care about them as well as giving them clear feedback. It's where the positive feedback element can again be useful.

From proving to improving

This wonderful phrase was coined by Chris Moyse, an education leader, trainer and consultant with over 30 years' experience working in schools. The shift in focus implied by this statement is exactly why the BASIC coaching method has such a strong focus on curiosity, positivity and growth. Organisations where performance management and appraisal are largely focused on judgment rather than personal development usually create a culture of defensiveness and negativity rather than one based on positivity and possibility.

The final chapter builds on this idea and will explore the second half of a productive feedback conversation: once someone has identified what they want to improve, how they can go about making change happen?

BASIC QUESTIONS

- ✓ I thought that … was really good. I particularly liked… What were you most pleased about?
- ✓ What have I missed that you thought went well?
- ✓ I'm curious about what you thought about…?
- ✓ What could have been even better about…?
- ✓ If you were doing this again, what would you want to change?
- ✓ So, you have decided you would like to improve on… What do you think you would like to do about this?
- ✓ How could you make that better?
- ✓ If you achieved this, how would you feel?
- ✓ What can I help you with on this?

 # BASIC REVIEW

- ✓ What are the disadvantages of the feedback sandwich?
- ✓ How does giving some positives before asking questions make people less defensive?
- ✓ What do you think of the 'Mind your Ps and Qs' idea?
- ✓ To what extent do you currently start with more open questions?
- ✓ How can you use closed questions to focus in on issues?
- ✓ Don't forget, if all else fails, it's absolutely fine to just tell them!
- ✓ What's been most useful about this chapter for you?

NOTES

15

Feed Forward

BASIC STEPS   BASIC QUALITIES   BASIC HABITS   **BASIC FEEDBACK**

MAKE CONNECTIONS   **FEED FORWARD**

This final chapter focuses on the second important part of a feedback conversation, which is sometimes overlooked. Once you have helped your coachee identify what it is they want to improve on, the next stage is to work out what they need to do. It's not usually that helpful when people offer feedback about what needs to change but don't then offer any support with what to do about it.

Should you coach or mentor?

As discussed in Chapter 10, your first step will usually be to see what ideas your coachee has about what they could do by *asking first*. If they are successful in identifying a strategy and potential actions, you are probably going to just carry on coaching in the way the rest of this book has outlined, helping them refine and develop their ideas.

However, if you can see they are struggling with a way forward and don't know what to do, that is the moment when you may wish to offer them the option of hearing any ideas you have, either by giving advice or showing them what to do. By doing this you will clearly be moving from coaching to mentoring on the continuum – you will be *feeding forward*.

Feed forward with instructional coaching

Taking this approach is not, let's be clear, in line with our first definition of coaching from Christian van Nieuwerburgh at the start of the book. When you are mentoring, the learning is not self-directed. For this reason, as we saw earlier, the BASIC definition of coaching is wider, allowing when necessary – and with a coachee's support – that move from coaching to mentoring.

BASIC coaching definition

> A one-to-one conversation that focuses on the enhancement of learning through increasing self-awareness and a sense of personal responsibility, where the coach facilitates the self-directed learning of the coachee, through questioning, active listening, appropriate challenge and, **when needed, practical guidance** in a supportive and encouraging environment **that leaves the coachee feeling clearer and more optimistic about the future**.

This modified approach, sometimes known as *instructional coaching*, has been growing in popularity in recent years because of the flexibility it offers. Thinking back to discussing *contracting*, this is one of the areas I always seek agreement on with my coachees before we start. As I mentioned before, when I contract it is always on the basis that I will *always ask first* but am happy, with my coachee's agreement, to move from coaching to mentoring if I think I can offer advice or demonstrate something which might be helpful.

To give an example, we are back for a final time to my conversations with my Uncle Peter. I can remember talking to him about paying his bills. For years he had always paid all his utility bills with cash at the Post Office. With his mobility reduced and his eyesight failing, this was becoming increasingly difficult. So, I asked him: 'What do you think you could do about this?' He said he thought there was probably some way of getting the bills paid directly from his bank account, but he didn't quite know how it all worked. At this point, I could have quite happily coached him into how he could find out how to do this. It would probably have involved phoning the utility companies and then his bank.

Just like you in this situation, of course I didn't do that. I simply asked him if he would like me to explain how it all worked, and then paused for him to think. I have learned with Peter that he sometimes needs thinking time, but it is always worth it in the end because he invariably comes back with a positive reply which means he is still on board with me. When I have just rushed in with advice, he has often started to feel like he is losing control and sometimes stops engaging.

Planning for success

The final recap I would like to offer is about how you can help your coachee make sure they have thought of everything they need to do before they embark on a plan of action. You may recall we explored John Kotter's change model in Chapter 4 on BASIC implementation.

 CREATE THE RIGHT CONDITIONS
✓ Be clear on your why
✓ Utilise a guiding team
✓ Create a powerful vision

 GET THINGS STARTED
✓ Launch the change
✓ Enable great action
✓ Create quick wins

 DELIVER GREAT RESULTS
✓ Get real time feedback
✓ Tackle your laggards
✓ Build into your systems and processes

You may choose to use the model to help your coachee draw up their plan. Or you may use it yourself to help frame your questions. For example, when it comes to getting things started, three key questions are relevant:

- What do you think is the best way to launch this change?
- What do you need to do to make sure everything will work smoothly?
- What do you think a really good quick win might look like with this?

As we come to the end of this chapter, I am reminded of the power of one of Michael Bungay-Stanier's seven questions: 'What's been most useful for you?' This a great question for you to use at the end of a coaching conversation, supporting your coachee to summarise what the positives are that they have taken from the dialogue and allowing them to focus on the key actions they are going to take going forward.

In the final part of the book, I will share a few parting thoughts about coaching as a personal and an institutional journey.

BASIC QUESTIONS

- ✓ You have identified that you want to be better at… What do you think you need to do?
- ✓ How do you think you can improve on that?
- ✓ What kind of situation does this issue arise in?
- ✓ What would this look like if you nailed it?
- ✓ What else could you do to improve this?
- ✓ What can I help you with?
- ✓ What has been useful about what I have shared with you?
- ✓ How are you going to make sure this becomes a long-term habit?
- ✓ What could go wrong with this idea?
- ✓ What can you do about that?
- ✓ Out of ten, how committed to this are you?

 # BASIC REVIEW

- ✓ Whilst the best feedback involves identifying areas for growth or improvement, it also includes support for subsequent actions – we call this feed forward. How can you see this working in your context?
- ✓ When it comes to identifying what needs to change, how easy do you find it to start by asking first, just to see how much your coachee can work out for themselves?
- ✓ If something is new or your coachee doesn't have the skills or experience needed, how will you know if it's OK to move into mentoring mode?
- ✓ Could you see yourself using Kotter's change model in some way to help your coachee structure an action plan?
- ✓ What has been most useful about this chapter for you?

NOTES

Final Thoughts

BASIC STEPS   **BASIC** QUALITIES   **BASIC** HABITS   **BASIC** FEEDBACK

In writing this book I have tried to distil all my own learning and experience of coaching from the last decade into a book that is easy to access, rooted in research and practical in its application. Whether you choose to use the BASIC method at work or at home, I do hope it will help you not only to structure conversations effectively but also to develop the habits and personal qualities that will make those conversations even more productive.

Coaching is a personal journey

One thing that has really struck me in writing this book is how my own coaching has grown and developed over time. It is a universal truth that there is always room for improvement, and this is certainly true with coaching. So long as we properly reflect, ideally with someone coaching us, we can always keep getting better in the way we coach. I hope this book will have given more experienced coaches, as well as those who are at the start of their coaching journey, some useful food for thought.

One of the things which is potentially tricky about coaching is how to get feedback on how well you are doing, not least because conversations are confidential and often about sensitive topics. One way, as I mention in the book, is to record yourself and just listen back. Of course, you will need your coachee's permission, particularly if you are going to review this with a coach of your own, but my own experience is that there is usually plenty to improve upon when we watch ourselves back.

Creating a coaching culture

This book is primarily aimed at helping individuals become better coaches, both at work and at home. However, when I received feedback during the writing process, one topic that came up a couple of times was about how one creates a culture of coaching in an organisation. I thought it might be useful to share a few high-level thoughts on this:

- You have to start with building trust. People need to see coaching as something that is an *entitlement*, something that individuals value and look forward to, not as something used by an organisation to rectify problems or 'fix' failing individuals.
- Leaders in an organisation need to be seen to value coaching; by taking part in formal coaching sessions for their own development, and by using a coaching approach in their everyday conversations, as described in this book.
- Where possible, confidential coaching should be offered by coaches who are external to an organisation, and in any event certainly not someone who is in the line management chain.
- Sometimes this can be achieved by partnering with other local organisations.
- From my own experience, schools are very good at doing this by using the many collaborative networks which exist within the educational sector.

- When you start, you might like to use Kotter's change model to plan the process.
- People need to understand the rationale for why coaching is being introduced.
- There needs to be time devoted to high-quality training;
- A shared understanding of what coaching is and isn't is really important.
- Regular evaluation of how the coaching is working should be built in.
- Success stories should be shared and celebrated.

Your own coaching journey

Whatever you have taken from this book, I hope it has given you some insight into the power of coaching to change our world for the better. From my own perspective, it has made me happier and more fulfilled at work and at home. I wish you the very best as you continue on your own coaching journey.

This is also the first book I have self-published. If you have found it useful, please do let your friends, family and colleagues know about it! If you would like to let me know what you liked, or if there are things you would like to suggest that I can incorporate into the next edition of the book to improve it, do email me.

Andy Buck
andy@honk.org.uk

Recommended Reading

BASIC STEPS   **BASIC** QUALITIES   **BASIC** HABITS   **BASIC** FEEDBACK

Achor, S. (2010) The happiness advantage: The seven principles of positive psychology that fuel success and performance at work. New York: Random House.

Bambrick-Santoyo, P. (2012) Leverage leadership. San Francisco: Jossey-Bass.

Brown, B. (2018) Dare to lead: Brave work. Tough conversations. Whole hearts. London: Vermilion.

Bungay-Stanier, M. (2016) The coaching habit: Say less, ask more and change the way you lead forever. Toronto: Box of Crayons Press.

Campbell, A. (2015) Winners: And how they succeed. London: Hutchinson.

Campbell, J. and Van Nieuwerburgh, C. (2018) A leader's guide to coaching in schools. Thousand Oaks: Corwin.

Downey, M. (2003) Effective coaching: Lessons from the coach's coach. London: Texere Publishing.

Goleman, D. (2017) Leadership that gets results. Boston: Harvard Business Review Classics.

Jackson, P. and McKergrow, M. (2002) The solutions focus: the simple way to positive change. London: Nicholas Brealey.

Kline, N. (2009) More time to think. London: Ward Lock.

Knight, J. (2017) The impact cycle: what instructional coaches should do to foster powerful improvements in teaching. Thousand Oaks: Corwin.

Kotter, J. P. (2012) Leading change. Boston: Harvard Business Review Press.

Scott, K. (2017) Radical candour: How to get what you want by saying what you mean. New York: St Martin's Press.

Starr, J. (2016) The coaching manual: The definitive guide to the process, principles and skills of personal coaching. London: Pearson.

Whitmore, J. (2009) Coaching for performance: Growing human potential and purpose - the principles and practice of coaching and leadership. London: Nicholas Brealey.

Acknowledgements

BASIC STEPS   **BASIC** QUALITIES   **BASIC** HABITS   **BASIC** FEEDBACK

There are so many people that have helped me with my learning and thinking about coaching. I am indebted to Andrea Berkeley, Anette Gray, Christian van Nieuwerburgh, Christine Drummond, Frances Matthews, Glyn Rawlins, Jim Knight, Jo Lewis, John Campbell, John Whitworth, Michael Bungay-Stanier, Myles Downey, Rachel Lofthouse, Steve Margetts, Tim Rutherford and Tim Stone for their excellent thinking, training and writing.

I should also like to thank my good friend, Peter Douglas, for proof-reading the book so effectively, casting his brilliant eye for detail and consistency over every inch of the book with such humility and humour.

Thank you, too, to all the family, friends, colleagues and Twitter followers listed overleaf who responded to my call for feedback on the first draft and who have all given generously of their time to offer support and feedback during the writing process. The response has been immense, and I have no doubt this is a much better book as a result.

Abby Bayford, Aidan Rossiter, Alaric Govan, Amir Arzoo, Andy Buffham, Becky Anderson, Ben Barton, Ben Layzell, Bill Jerman, Brendan Shanahan, Cathal Lynch, Catherine Cook, Charlotte Bartolomeo, Claire Hill, Claire Price, Claire Rohdie, Clementine Stewart, Dan Woodman, Darren Barton, David Cobb, Elizabeth Swan, Emma Grice, Emma Hopkins, Gemma Singleton, Gen Mitchell, Gerry Holden, Ian Gibson, Jane James, Joanna Buck, John Budden, John Crittenden, John Etty, Kat Howard, Kate Rumboll, Kerensa Healy, Laura Markendale, Laura Reader, Laura Watkin, Leonie Hurrell, Lizzie Mullarky, Lorna Good, Louise Hutton, Maggie Atkinson, Maggie Fidler, Martin Bayliss, Mary Lafferty, Matt Seex, Michael Pain, Michael Serridge, Michelle Prosser Haywood, Mike Buchanan, Natalie Jayne Aveyard, Nick Blackburn, Nick Heard, Nick O'Connell, Olivia Urso, Patsy Kane, Paul Sheehan, Peter Fairbrother, Richard Buckle, Richard Clutterbuck, Roger Higgins, Ros McMullen, Sarah Hanquinioux, Sarah Jerman, Sarah Mullin, Sarah Parekh, Shashie Harry, Sian Rowles, Simon Gould, Simon Jackson, Sue Plant, Thomas Kelly, Tim Rutherford, Tony Glover, Tricia Taylor and Wendy Buck.